THE SACRED . OU

First published in the UK in 2015 by
The Cloister House Press
This revised edition 2017

ISBN: 978-1909465411

THE SACRED YOU

Toby Negus

"The Sacred You is a beautiful book, made more so because it is obviously a reflection of the author's deep personal journey to find peace in the midst of painful circumstances. Filled with original artwork and teachings born of experience, this book is a gentle hand stretched out to guide the road weary into a new way of seeing the world and themselves."

Jacob Nordby - author of The Divine Arsonist: A Tale of Awakening and Blessed Are the Weird - A Manifesto for Creatives

ACKNOWLEDGEMENT

I would like to acknowledge all the great teachers of my life, both known and unknown, seen and unseen.

Above all I would like to acknowledge my heart who, when I have allowed it, has given me an endless supply of intelligence and love.

DEDICATION

This book is dedicated to you the reader that you may find and live the life you love.

CONTENTS

ABOUT THIS BOOK

This book is not a 'self help' book with lists of tasks and to do's, nor is it a deep complex picture of the inner workings of the spirit and the evolution of human consciousness. But it will enable you to help yourself by shedding light on the profound life that we are. It will explain in simple terms the faculties and powers that we have and how they work, enabling you to create the actions and attitudes that liberate who you love to be.

It is said that you can't teach anyone, you can only show them a picture and if they see meaning in it, they will then teach themselves.

It is not the lack of time or money that stops us from being who we wish to be, it is the lack of a tangible vision, a picture that touches our heart and opens the mind to the possibilities of life.

HOW IT BEGAN

This book started some years ago, when I was in a dark place in myself. I was feeling desperate, desolate, depressed and downright pissed off. I had tried everything I could that might offer freedom to the life I felt inside me. Over the years I had searched much of the ancient knowledge of the world and much of the new age understandings about the meaning of a spiritual life. I created hundreds of practices to help build my self-development; I had even beaten myself to a pulp with all the 'shoulds' and 'oughts' that those who proclaim to be developed recommend. But there was still something missing; I still felt unable to create the life I wished for myself.

I felt let down and alone, and the world outside offered no peace and no respite from the pain I felt.

I had nothing left, nowhere else to turn. I had only me. So I drove inwards into the very core of myself, to a place I had never been before, nor even knew existed. I embraced the deep unknown within me, without conditions or expectations because I had nothing left to give, nothing to clothe my pained, naked and vulnerable self. I did not find a monster or a place void of light. I found peace and felt, surprisingly, no longer alone.

In that moment I had somehow accepted all that I was: the good, bad and the ugly. In that settlement, I saw within me everything that I needed to be who I love. I understood that I was my own saviour and, of course, wished it to be no other way. I felt that I had somehow opened the final door.

THE FINAL DOOR

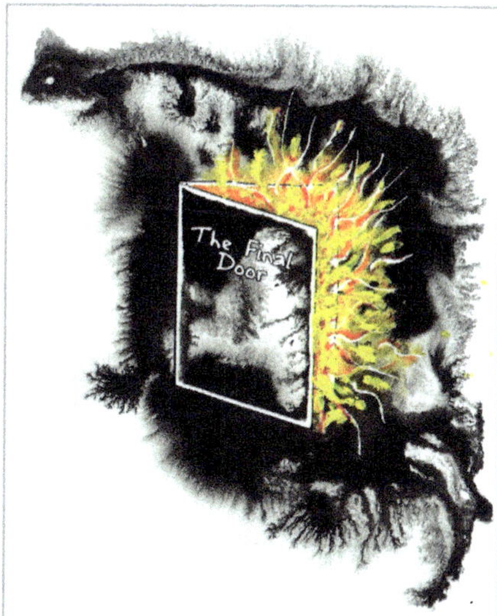

Know you are your own saviour.

I saw that there was no attitude that I could not summon, no aspiration I could not fulfil, if I chose it to be so.

We can, should we find a reason and a feeling to do so, create any attitude we want. We have the fundamental ability to create our life, to decide our purpose, chose what to think about and how to think about it. To decide the motive for our actions and the reasons why we do what we do. To choose what to do with the emotions that rise up in us because of our choices and our experiences.

Why should it be any other way?

Would we really want other people to be the authority for who we are?

After I saw that I was my own solution I could not understand why I had thought it should be any other way or why part of me was always looking outside to other people and things to be the provider of my happiness.

It was obvious that I was my own authority and that my authenticity was the only real way to release my loves in life.

Why do we assume that this is not the truth? Why do we think that other people and things have the answer, have authority over who we are?

I saw that the way of the world creates the idea that there is not enough time, money or love to be who we are, making sure that we look outside of ourselves for the answer to our happiness. I saw that the business and the commercial world creates an image of itself as the saviour, providing the things it says we need before we can be happy, ensuring that we always want more of what only it can provide. Even the culture of 'acceptable' social behaviour ensures that we want to be liked and look to other people for a confirmation of who we are.

I saw this as an illusion propagated by the money managers of the world and those who would have us believe that our sanity is in conforming to the expected norm.

Give up trying to get help from the outside

I knew that I had to give up the illusion that other people and things had the answer to who I was and to my happiness. And that trying to organise the world outside to be the solution was a dumb, impossible task.

Of course other people and things can provide great support and encouragement to life and this planet is a wonderful place to grow our expression of love. But unless our premise for action is drawn from within ourselves, from our own authenticity, we will forever be chasing the illusive 'more' to feel 'secure' in who we are and never find the peace and happiness that we know is our right.

Knowing you are your own saviour

To be saved by the perfect job, the wonderful partner, lots of money, fame, a new car or phone or a friendly look from someone we admire: all these things can be great but without the deep connection to self, their occurrence only provides temporary relief from the pain of our absence from ourselves. We are our own saviours. That is how we have been created. We have been endowed with a faculty that can, if we have the wit and will, focus our life on anything we choose. This is the fundamental gift of life and means that the authority for who we are does not lie outside of ourselves but, thankfully, lies in our hands.

THE SACRED YOU

The Power of the Mind and the Wisdom of the Heart

We are a phenomenal form of life. We have, within our mind, a godlike ability to create our life and give it meaning. We may think anything about anything we choose, we may define any reason for any action we do. Our mind is the crucible to the meanings we have given to our experiences and the purposes we have for why we do what we do. These meanings create our world.

We have also been graced with a touchstone for what is truly important, our heart. For it is to our heart that we will always return to find the truth of how we really feel and the place we will go to find our purpose in life.

These two sources of power and wisdom have all that we need to create the celebration of our life.

Heal the heart.

I have, for many years been a great 'head' person, thinking and logic with a spattering of intuition were my gods. I prided myself on my ability to hold powerful concepts in my mind, to understand why and how I thought. I was not heartless but I was not into the fluffy heart stuff that some people seemed to use as a substitute for being responsible for their lives.

But now, who I think I am has changed, where I go to touch the purpose of life is no longer the head.

Although the head is still a fantastic place to sort and organise my future, it is no longer my priority.

When all is said and done, what is really important? What is it that makes us feel deeply happy about ourselves? What is it that, above all, we cherish and what is it that we would not want to live without? Whatever the answer, it comes from the heart of us.

When we touch our own heart we liberate our will to join life at the very core of its meaning, to create a celebration of all that we hold dear. When we touch the heart in another we become part of the natural fire of life, all is forgiven and we become again a champion of the spirit that lives behind the eyes of all.

But the fire of the heart has been subdued by the gross demands of the 21st century. It has become closed and hardened by the teachers who have taught us who we should be and who have made unimportant things important.

The commercial world tells us that we are not 'enough', that we need more, bigger, better to be at peace and be happy with ourselves. The media has taught us that bad news is good news and that the trivialities of celebrities are really, really important. The business world has taught us that money is important and that whoever has the most is the winner and all the rest are losers. Society has taught us to hide the truth of ourselves (never say what we really feel) and to act the part of 'normality' as expected by all of the above. And that other people's view of us is more important than our view of ourselves.

So we close our heart...

So we close our heart to who we are in an attempt to be what we are told we should be.

So we harden our heart...

So we harden our heart trying to get the things that the world says are important to be happy.

We suppress our heart...

We suppress our heart, not saying what we really feel, not saying what we want to hear, but saying what we think others want to hear.

My heart may get bruised, beaten and broken but, I can still feel the knowing in my heart about the purpose of life that I had when I was very young, and I can see it in the eyes of any young child at play. Like them I wished only to express the loves the deep of me felt about life. It wasn't complicated or obscure. I knew I needed nothing more than who I was to be part of life.

As a child my mind had not been molested by society's expectations so there was little distraction in my response to life; it was unfettered, full and heartfelt; there was little I could not imagine or do. Naïve it may have been, but it was an honest response to the loves I felt about life.

This was before the world taught me that I was not enough, that there was not enough time, money or love to be who I wished to be, before my innocence was replaced with a cynical judgment of others and myself, and before my natural intuition to explore the unknown was replaced with brittle conditions of how things should or should not be.

Now that I am older, my will to express what lies within my heart has become haunted by the fear and anxiety that have grown up in me in my attempt to live in a world that seems callous and indifferent to the grace of life I once felt.

We still hold the knowledge of deeper life inside ourselves, often only known by our intuition. It prompts us toward the deeper love we have about life. It always comes to light when we are quiet enough in ourselves to allow the memory of who we really are to be felt.

Talk gently to yourself about

what you truly care about.

So you will know

who you really are.

BEING HUMAN

I love it when I am feeling whole, settled and happy with my life, when I feel inspired about who I wish to be. My life makes sense and the world seems to play its part in my vision.

But these times can be rare. I can find myself just trying to cope with who I have become and what I think the world is throwing at me.

We are complex beings experiencing thousands of thoughts and hundreds of different emotions every day. It can feel like a bizarre task being a human, with a cauldron of stuff going on inside us: our thoughts, emotions, habits and many other parts of us that, at times, seem to be partying at our expense. If someone pushes the wrong button in us an emotional explosion or implosion can occur on what was a sunny day. We may be as sweet as pie with our loved one but within the hour we can be foul-mouthed to another car driver.

Living in a Game of Chance

We may install a new sweet government in our heads, composed of sanity, heart and careful plans, on a Sunday but by Monday afternoon the government has been overthrown by a bitter dictator, no longer listening to the vision of our hearts, declaring war on anything that is not compliant to its aim to win at any cost!

These changes of attitude can seem like a game of chance because of the multiple combinations between what we are dealing with, what emotions we are doing it with and why we are doing it; what purpose or motive is moving us.

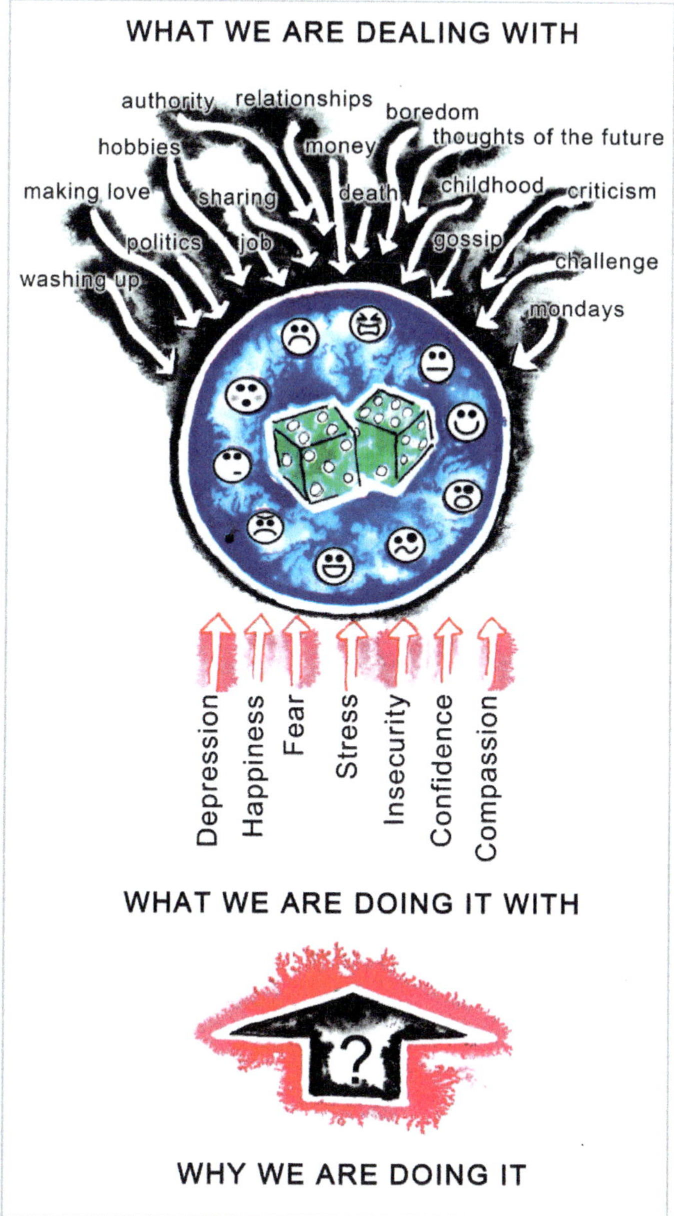
WHAT WE ARE DEALING WITH
authority
relationships
boredom
hobbies
money
thoughts of the future
making love
sharing
death
childhood
criticism
politics
job
gossip
challenge
washing up
mondays
Depression
Happiness
Fear
Stress
Insecurity
Confidence
Compassion
WHAT WE ARE DOING IT WITH
?
WHY WE ARE DOING IT

Building a Picture

So how do we make sense of the 'who we are' that is doing what we do? How can we discern the core parts of ourselves? Can we create a simple picture that helps us understand who we are and why we do what we do?

Where do we start?

Oh! .... Here I am!

The starting point of who we are is our consciousness. Without it we would not be aware of ourselves and life. It is our consciousness that gives us our awareness – our awareness of the weather, a smile from another person and how we are feeling in ourselves.

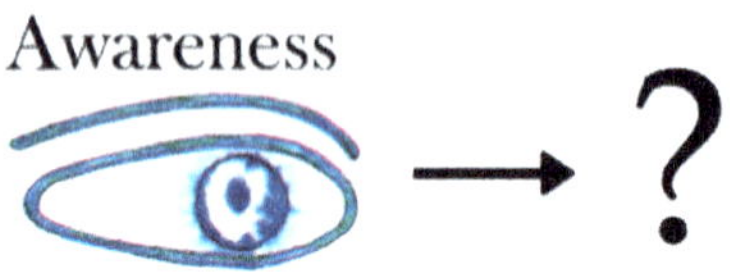

What influences our awareness and where does it come from?

Our attitude determines how we interpret what we see and our attitude is caused by our state of mind. A positive mind will create positive attitudes and will see things to be positive about!

What makes up our mind? What causes us to become mindful and aware of one thing and not another?

It's what's important to us that fills the mind, be it money, social acceptability or our inner well-being. We become mindful about it because of what it means to us. Why it means something to us can be as unique to us as our fingerprints. But whatever the reasons, they become the driving force that creates our attitudes and determines our awareness.

What builds our reasons, the 'why do we do what we do'?

So what are the main creators and instigators of why we do what we do? The biggest players are our thoughts (thinking), and our feelings (emotions). What we think about and what we feel about it create and flavour the meanings we give to life. They create the story we tell ourselves about who we are and create the meaning of our life.

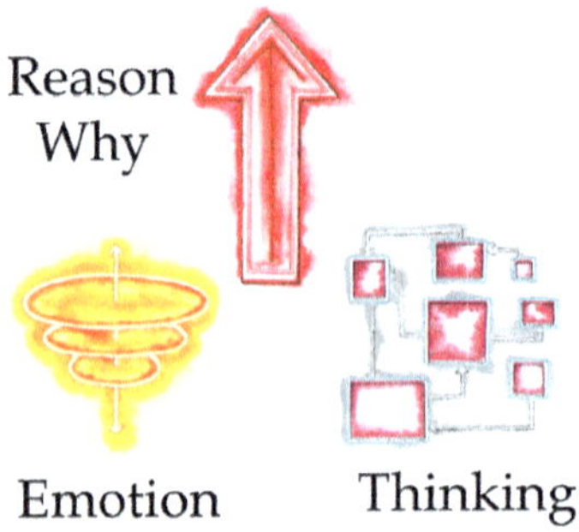

What are the main influences on our thinking and emotions?

Our history of experiences, the thinking and emotional habits we have created and the beliefs that have been created because of these habitual thoughts and emotions.

These are the parts of ourselves that make the decisions about who we are and what we may become. They are highly integrated and react to each other.

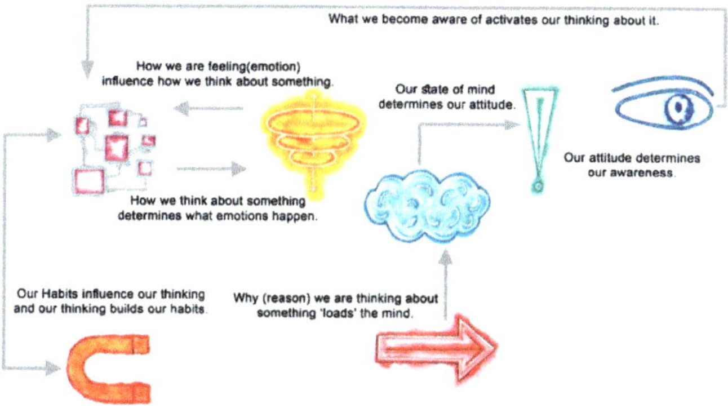

They can, as an example, in a fraction of a second, go through the following process.

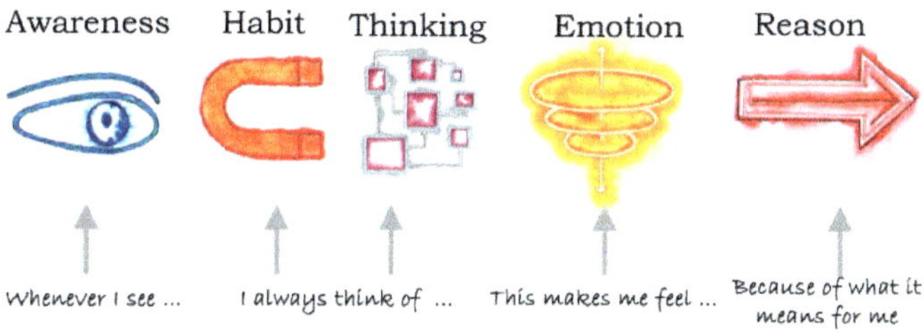

THE HEROES & VILLAINS

These elements are the heroes and villains because sometimes they save us and sometimes they steal from the life we wish to live.

They are the resources that we have within ourselves, the power of the emotions, the strength of habit, the significance of our attitudes, the driving force of why we do what we do. They have a deep effect on how we see the world, what we feel is possible, how we respond to the heart of ourselves and to the world outside of us.

Be they hero or villain, we have made them so and may learn who we are because of them.

They are the servants to our life, but they can only serve us according to how we have educated them. We teach them by what we think about, why we think what we think and what we do with the emotions that arise in us because of our experience.

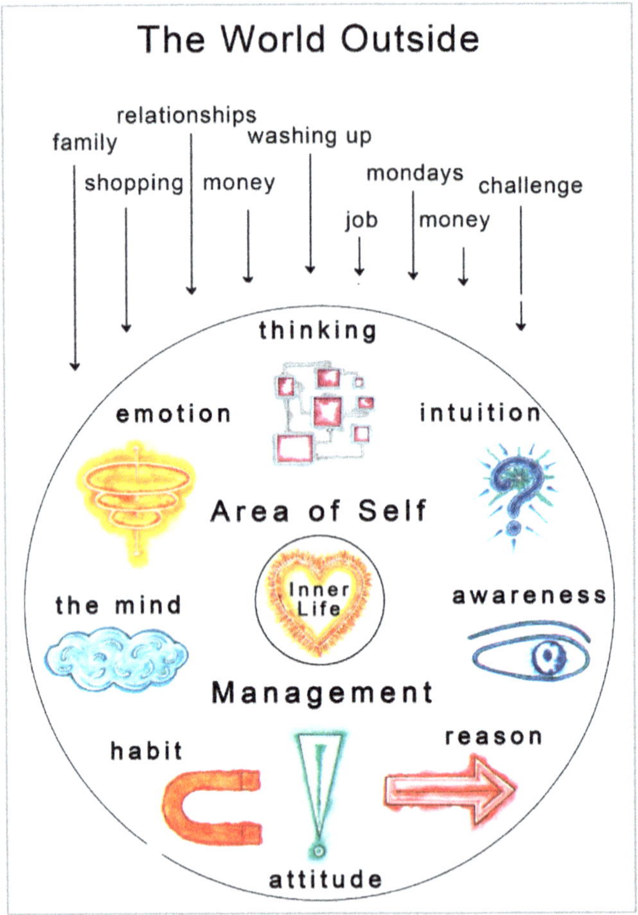

These and our faculty of intuition, are the parts of ourselves that we have at our disposal to manage the world outside and to serve our heart's purpose.

Each element can be both hero and villain. It is often our sense of fragility that evokes our villains and our willingness to allow our vulnerability that allows our heroes.

If we are feeling fragile we become closed and cannot accept our vulnerability, if we are feeling vulnerable, we have moved into the unprotected part of our self and have the choice whether we feel fragile about it.

The Fragile Villain

When I move into the villain of myself it is often because I feel fragile, as if I were not enough, as if I could be broken. So I close off and become superior or inferior to whatever caused the fragility to appear. I let go of who I love to be and go to what I know is secure. I become the judge and the jury naming and shaming myself and all that I see as right, wrong, good, bad, better or worse – as if I knew it all!

The Vulnerable Hero

When I am in the hero of myself I may feel magnificent but I also feel a sense of vulnerability, I feel exposed, no longer sheltered by my conditions on how I think things should be. I become willing to accept my imperfections and step forward, often nervously, into the unknown moment.

Following is a set of graphical illustrations of the villain and hero roles the elements in our area of self-management can play. In the next chapters, we will explore each of these areas in turn.

THINKING

THE ENGINEER

Our thinking builds the roads and bridges of our associations as to 'what goes with what'.

Hero **Creates our web of understanding, upon which we collect our perceptions.**

Sometimes my thinking travels along paths of sublime light, dancing in the profound meanings in all that I see, weaving pictures from the truths of what goes with what. What a clever machine you are! What a wonderful storyteller you are on my journey!

Villain **When our thoughts disturb who we wish to be.**

I can't stop my thinking – sometimes I wish I could, it just rattles on and on about things that I no longer wish to know about, it tells me stories about myself and other people that just give me grief. It's like it just doesn't care about me! Like it's a strange entity with its own agenda in life!

Learning **We are not our thoughts but we do go where they take us!**

I have learnt, as much as I can, to watch my thoughts, to be aware of how my thinking is thinking, what it is thinking and what it thinks about because of what it is thinking. This focus allows me to take greater care of myself and where possible, instigate new thinking so my thinking has healthy paths to follow, and more useful connections of what goes with what.

We have over 60,000 thoughts running around in our heads every day. From the thoughts we have about going to work to the thoughts we take to bed. Our thinking never stops building our view of the world, confirming our associations of what we think goes with what.

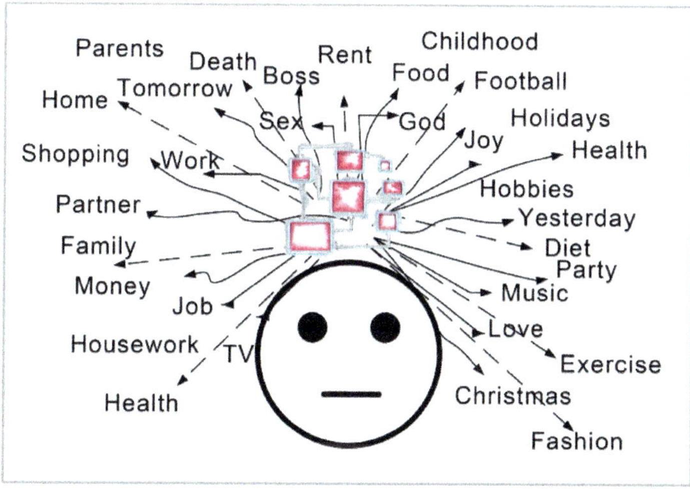

The world is a busy place and we have been given thousands of things to think about in order to navigate the world and the wants its teachers say we ought to have in order to be accountable to their expectations.

This collection and reference process is influenced by emotion (how we are feeling in ourselves), habit (our history of associations we have already made) reason/purpose (why we are doing what we are doing)

The job of our thinking is to diligently confirm the associations that we have told it are important. If we have taught it that Mondays are gloomy it will look to confirm this view by finding things to think about that help create the gloomy Monday we expect.

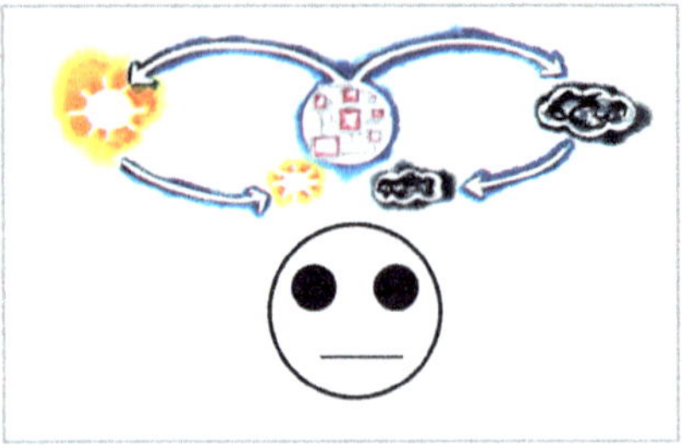

Thinking can make a good day better and a bad day even worse. It's not personal. It's just doing its job.

What we think about, and
why we think it, creates our view of the world.

If it didn't matter what we thought then these 60,000 thoughts would not matter. But what we think about and how we think about it has created who we think we are.

How we think about ourselves has created who we think we are. Who we think we are determines what we think is possible.

Of all the things we think about, how we think about ourselves has got to be one of the most important: it determines who we think we are and is made by the stories we tell ourselves about our life. These stories then determine:

- What clothes we wear, what food we eat.
- How we walk and how we talk.
- What we recall from our past and plant in our future.
- What friends we have and how much we smile.
- How much we give and how much we take.
- How we love and what we fear.

We become what we think about.

We attract to ourselves whatever goes with the frequency, tune and flavour of our thoughts.

- If we think about what we hate we will become hateful.
- If we think about what we love we will become lovable.
- If we think about unimportant things we will become unimportant.
- If we think about ourselves all the time we will become selfish.
- If we think about what we have not got we will become empty.

But we also cannot become what our thinking does not allow.

- We cannot feel gratitude if we think we are owed a life.
- If we think too much about what other people think of us we will never care enough how we think about ourselves.
- If we think we need 'more' to be who we are we will never find peace.
- If we only think about all the pain that is going on in the world we will never see the love that is being created.

Thinking and Habit

Thinking the same thoughts about the same things

Most of our thinking is habitual. It runs along in the background making its associations of what we have taught it belongs with what, repeating the same thoughts about the same things that we thought yesterday.

We can wake up in the morning with a clean slate about our life and what we think is possible. But after

30 minutes of habitual thinking, we re-recreate our old view of ourselves and the world.

Thinking and Emotion

The more we think about it, the more we feel.
The more we feel, the more we think about it.

Our thinking and emotions are so interconnected that it can be difficult to know where one starts and the other ends. But they are separate parts of us. The thinking is the circuitry and the emotions are the power flowing through the circuitry.

Our thinking evokes our emotions.

Our thinking evokes our emotions according to the meanings we have about what we are thinking about. These meanings will either bring what we describe as good, bad or ugly emotions. All according to the decision we have made about 'what goes with what'. What goes with relationships, money, going to work or even death.

Our emotions power our thinking.

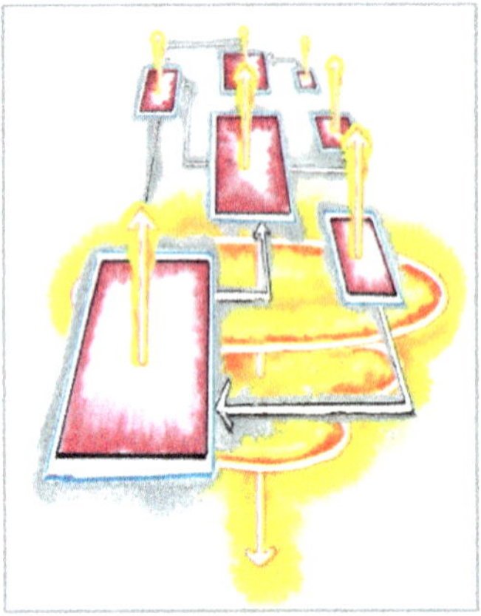

The greater the emotion the more we think about it.

Our thinking uses emotion to understand what is important to us: the greater the emotion, the more the importance, the more the thinking will give us things to think about it. These emotions may have been created from childhood experiences or from what happened yesterday; whatever they are, they become the signposts that guide our thinking, telling it how to think about things, what routes to take in the labyrinth of our associations of 'what goes with what'.

The job of your thinking is then to follow the signposts of importance that have been created by the emotions.

You become what you think about,
so take care that your thoughts do not
jeopardise your well-being, for your well-being is
paramount.

Thinking Through Time and Space

Our thinking is not constrained by time in its pursuit of its duty. It wanders into our yesterdays rummaging in the experiences of our past, bringing us back pictures and feelings that become the stories we tell ourselves about 'who we are'.

It fumbles into our future with all the things we will or won't do, all the things that might or might not happen, bringing us back the hopes and fears of what we expect tomorrow will be.

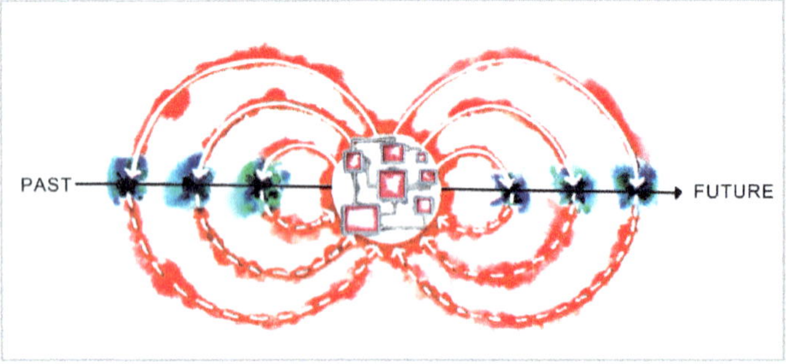

We go where our thinking goes. But what it brings back depends on why we sent it there in the first place.

The past is not dead nor the future unknown; it is a living timeline, changing according to our thoughts about it. We define our past and our future by how we think about them, and we can, if we have the will, change the feelings we receive from them by changing the stories we tell ourselves about who we are.

The Gentle Art of Self-awareness

What would we know about ourselves if we were able to spend a day watching ourselves thinking what we think, without judgment or condemnation upon ourselves or the subject of our thoughts?

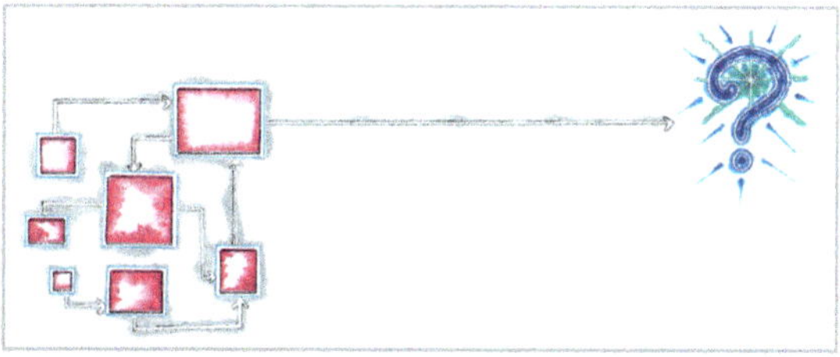

Creating an awareness of our thinking is tricky; it is not easy separating ourselves from the feelings that happen because of our thinking. And because we have so many thoughts every day, we draw our sense of identity from our thoughts. We think we are our thoughts but we are not – they are just the chattering story we tell ourselves about what we think is or is not happening, what we think has and has not happened and what we think will or will not happen in our lives.

Knowing what we are thinking is not half as important as knowing where our thinking goes because of what we think about. What we think about when our job, our partner, our home, our life comes to mind. These thoughts tell us much about what is moving in us that hour, day, year, life.

There is a great freedom and knowledge available for us if we can learn to separate ourselves from our thoughts, learn to be an observer of the thoughts, not reacting to them by jumping on them with emotion, but instead just watching them come and go across our consciousness, doing its associations of what we have taught it goes with what.

The more we create mindfulness about our thinking, the more we have a chance to escape the fixed view of ourselves that our thinking has created in its service to us. This freedom allows us to realise that we can think anything about anything we want.

We do not think in the now, we live in it.

When all is said and done, thinking is a tool to be used as such; it should not be running riot with our attempt at living. We often think too much and most of it, if not all of it, concerns either the past or the future – this disables our attempt to live in the now, for we do not think in the now, we live in it.

I think therefore I am not.

Our thinking is an after or before event, either thinking 'what will' or 'what has'. It does not happen when we are within the moment of the now. The experience of the now is a total experience that has no space for thinking, as soon as we think about what is happening we move away from the moment and use our history (habit) and reason to give it meaning; useful as this may be, we curtail the experience of the now by our need to name all that we do and see.

Thinking builds the grid upon which our consciousness sits.

Thinking	**The Engineer**
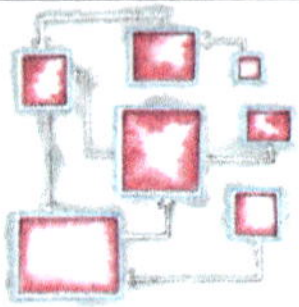	*Creates the bridges and pathways of our associations: 'what goes with what'*
Hero	*Creates our web of understanding, upon which we collect our perceptions.*
Villain	*When our thoughts disturb who we wish to be.*
Learning	*We are not our thoughts but we do often go where they take us!*

EMOTION

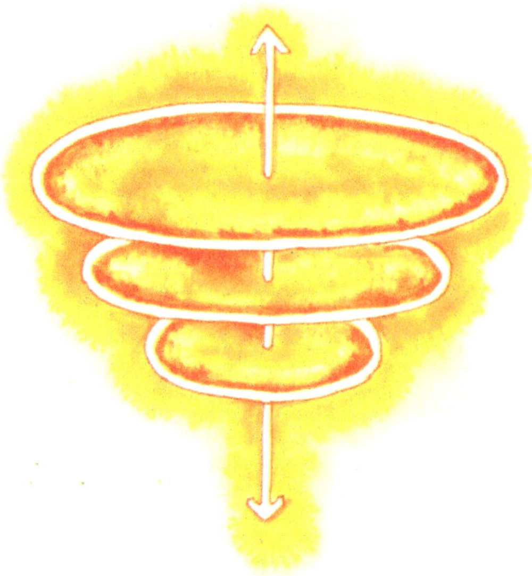

The Mover

Emotions are the fuel we are running on, the feelings we get from the energy that is moving through us. They tell us 'who' we are being.

Hero **Powers our intentions, purpose and will.**

What glory my emotions shower me with and what powerful visions they reveal by their presence! They heal my very soul with their warmth and light and I feel blessed.

Villain **When our emotions cause us to be someone we do not love.**

Oh, horrible me! How can I smile when the whole world does not care? When everything I see is as meaningless as the life within me? How can I lift myself up when I can't even raise my head, tread lightly when my feet are unable to move, stuck in everything that is not right?

Learning **Whatever we are feeling, it is us, we may learn from it.**

The emotions that cause me trouble will always be around, but I do not blame myself too much now for having them. Sometimes they make my road a bit bumpy, sometimes they make me crash. I know they are a part of me that is in pain. So if the pain is not too much or I am strong enough, I absorb the pain that they bring and look to cherish the part of me that is suffering. Sometimes I'm not strong enough to care and try to go elsewhere until the pain goes away. But I will not forget their call for help.

Emotion – The Mover

Our emotions move us throughout our day; we have hundreds of emotions about thousands of things every day. They lift us up and pull us down on our journey of learning about who we are.

They let us know how we feel about ourselves, what we feel about our yesterdays and how we feel about our tomorrows.

The Power of Emotions

They are a powerful force in our lives. Anger can be terribly destructive, and happiness is a fantastic gift to us and to others. Our emotions can leave us feeling tired and drained or fill us with well-being. They can give us courage in the face of adversity or they can fix us in fear.

We have so many emotions they can often seem chaotic, taking us on a roller-coaster ride of highs and lows. They can change in an instant because of a bill, a text or even a look that someone gives us. Our well-being can be lifted on a Friday and dashed on a Monday.

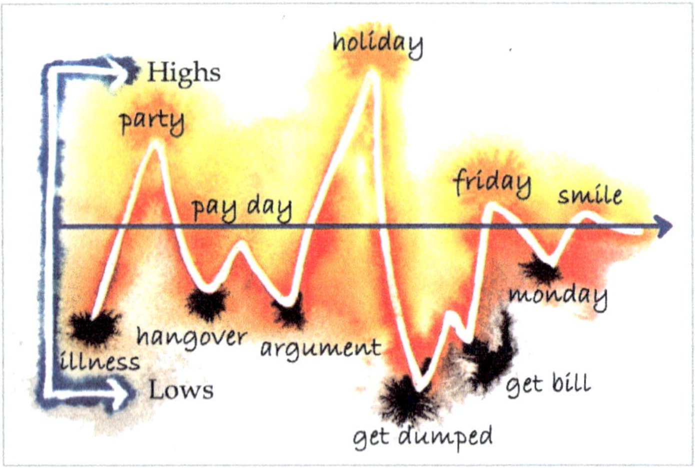

Travelling on this roller coaster can cause our purpose to end up being getting the highs or avoiding the lows. And the commercial world is happy to make millions from us by providing products that either help get the highs or anesthetize the feelings of the lows.

So much of our awareness is spent on what our feelings are causing in us; we have little time to understand the cause of the emotion. Not what person or thing caused them but what it was in us that allowed them to happen in the first place.

We may have sadness because we lost our job, we may have happiness because we found some money. It is the thinking that happens because of what happens that causes our emotion.

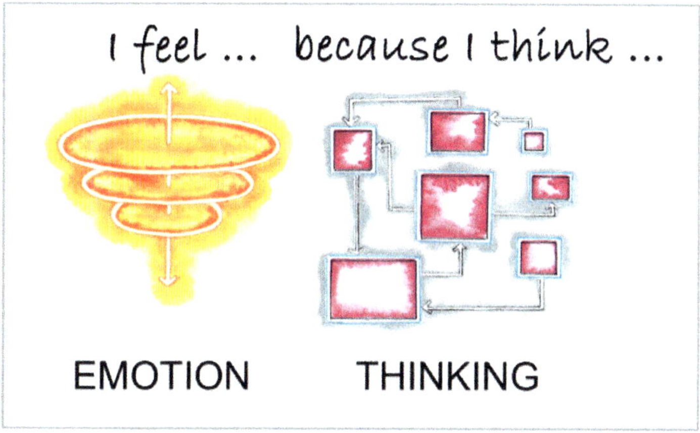

We have given permission to our feelings to appear by how we have decided to think about something.

It is how we think about our experience that determines the emotions we feel. If we want to know why we are feeling some emotion we need to go to the cause (our thinking) and the meaning we have about it.

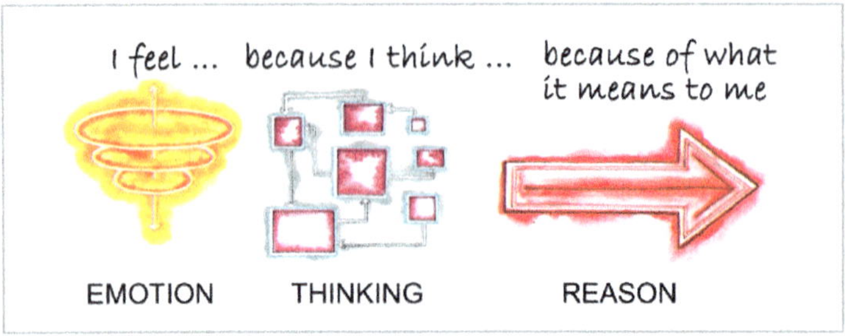

We are often aware of the people and incidents that triggered our emotions: a traffic jam, a bill, an argument. But it is the meanings we give to our experience that determines how we feel about it. It's what it means for us that matters. Two people can have the same experience, loss of a limb, losing a job, seeing a sunset, but can have different feelings about it because of the meanings they have about it.

The meanings we have given to our experience over the years have given us thousands of 'think-feel' reactions waiting for the opportunity to produce some emotions in us.

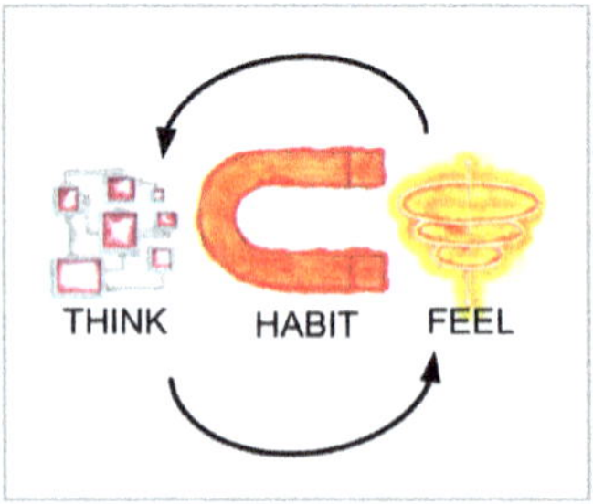

We have hundreds of these habitual 'think-feel' associations going on throughout our day. We may no longer be conscious of them; they just fire off whenever a certain subject or experience happens.

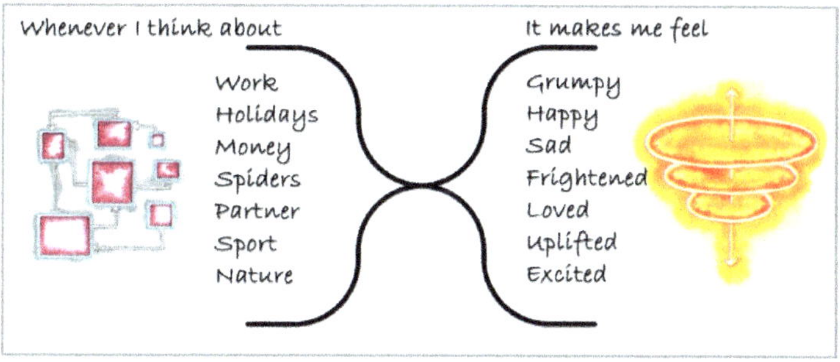

I think about ... because I am feeling ...

Our thoughts are also activated according to how we are feeling. We have sad thoughts when feeling sad, happy thoughts when feeling happy.

The chain reaction

What we are currently feeling is the tip of the iceberg of what is going on in us. Below our current emotion is the 'what we were thinking about' that caused the feelings. Below that is the 'why' we were thinking it in the way that caused the emotions, why it's important for us. Below that are the beliefs and conclusions we have built about our current experience.

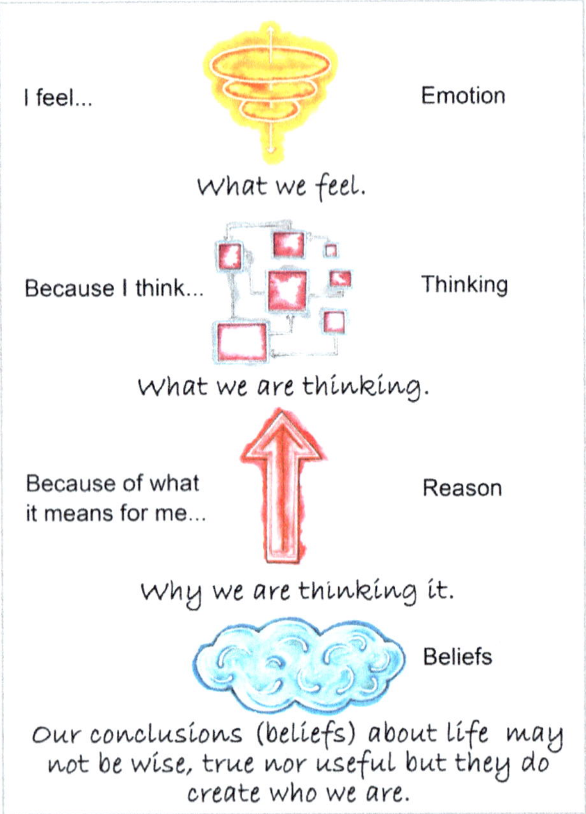

The meaning we have about our experience is rooted in our history; from childhood to our experiences yesterday we have built and confirmed the meanings we have about life. They may not be true, they may not be relevant to today but they power our todays.

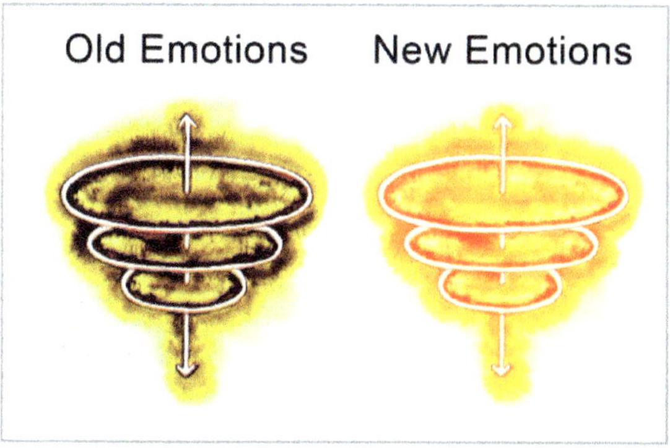

New emotions are born of the moment because of the moment and old emotions appear in the moment because of our yesterdays.

Old Emotions

When we act because of our yesterdays, we mess up the canvas of our todays with colours that are no longer bright.

We carry many great feelings from our history that bless our moments. But we have also developed ghosts that haunt our todays, such as all the hurts we have failed to forget and all the feelings we have suppressed, avoided and denied in ourselves. These are old emotions that come from the unloved parts of our self.

These emotions happen in the moment because of yesterday's feelings. When they appear they often display as childlike tantrums or teenage sulking, causing us, like an exasperated parent, to admonish and find ways to suppress them yet again.

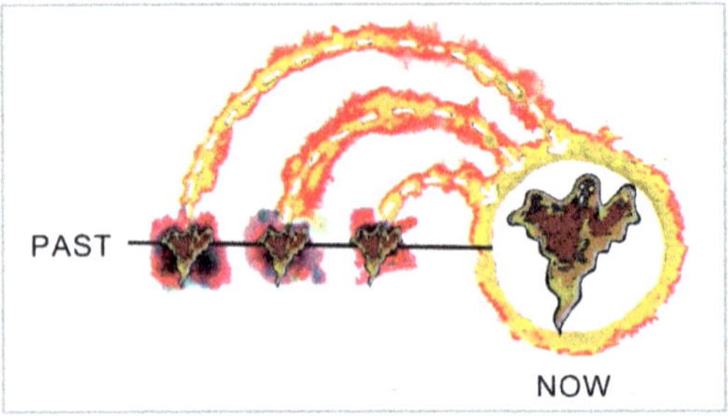

Our old emotions are always ready to put yesterday's emotions on today's experience. But whenever we manage to free ourselves and step into the moment of the now without conditions, we become refreshed and made new by the feelings we experience.

New Emotions

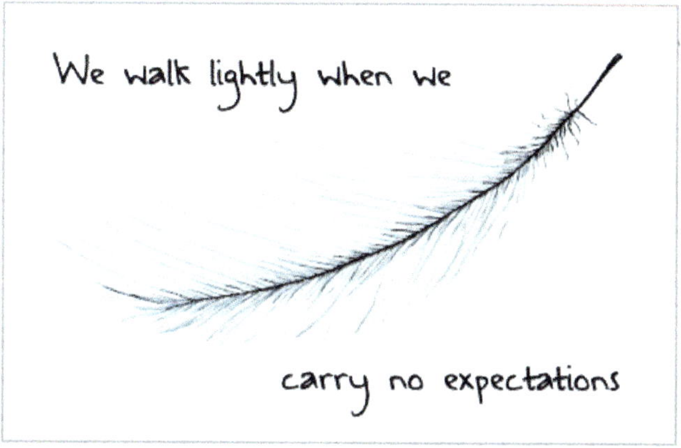

These are of the moment, because of the moment. They are a natural response to what we feel about life at the time. They do not carry stigma, judgment or conditions about whoever they are given to, nor to our self. They are given in response to what is happening at the time, and once given are then released without conditions.

Feelings in response to a beautiful sunset or seeing the joy of a young child are of the moment; only those who have developed a thick skin from years of self-denial cannot feel warmed and enlightened by such experiences.

These emotions are always available to us when we find ourselves uncluttered by our yesterdays and not suppressed by our tomorrows; they often carry feelings of gratitude and celebration of life and have the power to help heal any bruises we may feel life has given us.

The Good, the Bad and the Ugly

I have learnt that who I am is the all of me, the good, bad and the ugly. So I forgive myself often for the parts of me that do not seem to care about my well being.

But if I am hurting too much I will try to abandon my fear and feel the 'not good' of me so I can offer it cherishment. If the hurt is too much I will look for distraction until such time as my courage returns, then I will look for ways to heal the unloved part of me.

We can't expect to find peace
if we are at war with ourselves.

We are not very good at handling the whole truth of ourselves, the good, bad and the ugly. When our emotions cause us to be someone we do not love, we hide the truth of ourselves with suppression, avoidance, blame or any of the many drugs of distraction that the commercial world has available. In doing this we deny who we are, we forget the whole truth of ourselves. So when the inevitable happens - when things happen that bring to light our ghosts - we become surprised, upset, and distraught as if we didn't know they were there! We then re-enter the battle to again suppress or forget the whole truth of ourselves, the good, bad and the ugly.

When our emotions cause us to be someone we do not love, think of them as a child that needs care and understanding.

The Good – Calls for Gratitude and Sharing

These are the creative emotions. They make us feel happy, inspired and willing to share our life with others. They are the ones that allow us be who we love to be. They make us feel good about ourselves and the world, bringing optimism and clarity about our purpose in life.

When we stop being who we are and do not express the natural ebb and flow of our feelings, when we dam ourselves up by blocking the river of our feelings in our attempt at being perfect (or perfect in the eyes of another), then these feelings become part of the pain of who we are not!

The Bad – Calls for Learning

When we are at war with our ghosts...

These emotions can appear to be destructive and can make us feel unhappy, sad, depressed, lost or uncertain about who we are. We name them as 'bad' because they appear opposed to the good emotions that we love.

If we feel what we are feeling,
it has a message for us.

Many of the feelings we have been taught are 'bad' have within them an opportunity for learning and change. Grief is an important part of letting go, sadness can help us re-evaluate our values, regret can give us learning for the future, anger can be a powerful ally for change and in despair great resolution can happen.

It is only when we fail to get the learning that our 'bad' emotions are telling us that they then become ugly

The Ugly – Calls for Healing

When pain rules the day...

The ugly can often be rooted in early life experiences and then compounded over the years with our unresolved emotions about them. These are emotional reactions to things that either cause a violent explosion towards others or a violent implosion toward ourselves. These types of emotions require healing with professional help or sincere compassion to the self.

Truth and Reconciliation

Sometimes we just need to forget and sometimes we need to forgive before we can forget.

I don't always like who I am, in fact sometimes I am totally pissed off about who I am being. I don't know where I got the idea that I should be perfect but it has played havoc with

my life, but that's OK now. Because when I see it, I forgive myself.

Blame is often the first response when things go wrong instead of what we think is right. And it is accepted in society to blame other people or things for the feelings that happen in us. So we look to the world outside of us to understand why we are feeling what we are feeling, to save us from our pain. This is neither wise, true nor useful.

Blaming others is giving away our authority, blaming ourselves is to go to war with our very self.

When we take responsibility for our actions we heal the cause; when we blame ourselves for our actions we do not.

Whatever we are feeling it is part of the truth of who we are. The cause may be the love of the moment or it may be lost in the labyrinth of our memories. Whatever it is, we have, for whatever reason, given them permission to appear.

Some people can spend their whole life holding onto the pain they feel someone has given them. But I can often forgive quickly because I usually see the hell they are in that caused them to do it. Where I have struggled is forgiving myself. Oh, how I have given myself grief, poor me, how stupid! It may be because of my age or but I now seem more able to accept who I am and value my well-being more than the need to be right.

Of all the emotions we have in life, there is one that is most sacred, most worthy of care and one that we should not be timid about. It opens the heart and frees our mind, heals the past and lightens the future. There is not much it can't accomplish when it is set free.

It doesn't have to be perfect, it just has to be the love you feel.

Emotion	**The Mover**
	*Emotions are the fuel we are running on, the identity we give to the energy that is moving through us.*
Hero	*Powers our intentions, purpose and will.*
Villain	*When our emotions cause us to be someone we do not love.*
Learning	*Whatever we are feeling, it is us, and we may learn from it.*

HABIT

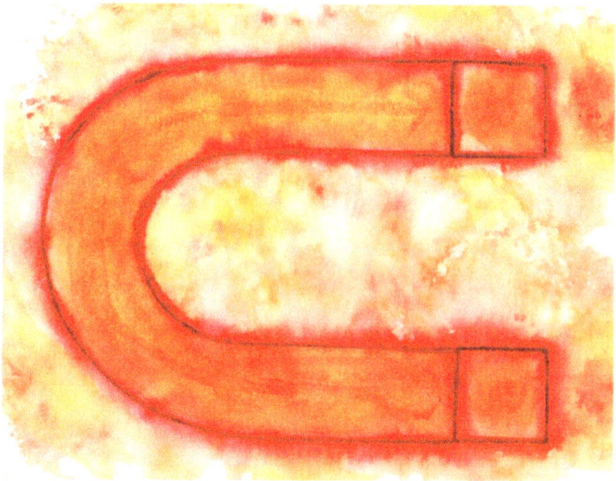

THE MAGNET

Habit is the automated response to life according to our personal history. The habit looks to ensure that our todays conform to our expectations and our prejudices.

Hero **Glorious engine that will run without thought anything we repeatedly do.**

Oh, what a faithful servant! I can wake up, get to the door, dressed and fed without even having to think about it! It gives me actions and attitudes during the day that confirm who I love to be. What a powerhouse it is for my purpose!

Villain **When our habits propel us into our tomorrows with yesterday's meaning.**

I really can't be bothered, I want a sign around my neck saying 'Do not disturb!' It always ends up the same! It's like some massive, bloody magnet dragging me back to who I don't want to be.

Learning **Just repeatedly do what you want to become.**

I have learned to forgive myself for not jogging and meditating as much as I think I should. I have learned that creating small, simple habits are the best way for me to remember what I don't want to forget.

Our habits draw us like a magnet to old ways of thinking and doing things. They are in our blood, the place we go for the comfort of the known.

We like the familiar, the routine, the regular things we do each day. It gives us a sense of security in an ever-changing world. Thank God for habits, for without them we would never be able to get dressed in the morning, drive a car or any of the hundred things they do for us each day.

But the habit is a hungry beast and will look to get involved in all aspects of our life. It will influence our thoughts when we wake up, how we think about money, our view of people and what we feel about ourselves. It sits as a powerhouse within us making us rigid and fixed in what, why and how doing things. It looks to ensure that our todays meet the expectations and conditions of how we think things should be.

The Habit – The Magnet

Our thinking, emotions and even the reason why we do things can all fall under the power of habit.

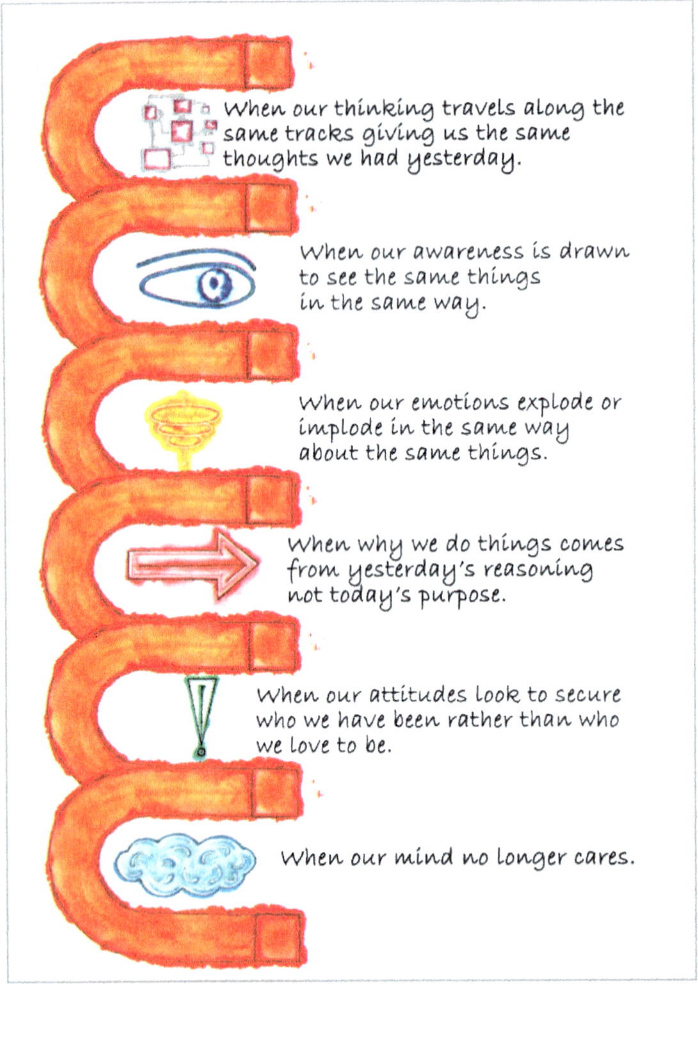

Our thinking, emotions and even the reason why we do things can all fall under the power of habit. This is great if the habits we have created support who we wish to be. But often our habits are just repeating our yesterdays with no care for our tomorrows.

Most of our thinking is habitual. We rarely see today as it is, just the picture of today painted from the pallet of yesterday's colours.

Once we have completed a cycle of learning, it is passed to habit to become fixed and repeated.

Whenever we move into a new situation, a new home, relationship or a new level of awareness, we like to know and get used to where the rooms are, what the person is like, how the new situation works, what can and cannot be expected. This enables us to be comfortable in it and not be shocked by things that fall outside of our expectations. After this interesting, 'getting used to the situation' stage, the situation is passed to habit for automation, causing us to slip into a familiarity with the person, place or thing, taking it for granted and therefore ceasing to learn.

The natural balance to our habitual life is our life of exploration, curiosity, learning and gratitude, but this life has taken a beating by the teachers who have taught us who we are. They have turned our curiosity about life into an appetite for commercial commodities. Our learning has mostly been reduced to learning for the sake of income. Our gratitude has been lost in the chase for the 'more' that they say we need.

Our life of exploration and adventure
has been curtailed

by the education from our teachers

who would have us believe that our sanity lies in conforming to the expected norm.

Making and Breaking Habits

Habits are very 'sticky' and once created are tough to alter or change. We will almost always be drawn back to our old way of doing things. The habit will resist change and will get sulky and grumpy if its old ways are challenged. But habit is just another part of our 'management of life' that can be understood and trained to assist who we wish to be. Educating the habit may not be easy but it is simple: just do it long enough so it becomes attractive to the habitual process.

Habit can be a powerful ally in helping us remember what we don't want to forget but can, just as easily, be the engine that causes us to remember what we want to forget.

What we are thinking or feeling while we are doing a habitual action can become woven into the physical habit process, making it easy for it to reappear next time we are doing the habit. We may have done this unconsciously with the habitual feelings we get when we wake up on a Monday morning or when we open the door to our place of work.

Evoking gratitude and linking affirmations to habitual actions

We have hundreds of habitual actions during the day, from getting out of bed to eating food, any one of which can be used to create a new think-feel association that brings us closer to who we love to be; over time the habitual action will automatically produce the attitudes we have asked for.

Changing the Reason behind the Habit

Why we do what we do is a crucial part of our authenticity and a powerful tool for making our purpose conscious and in creating our future. All the actions we take during the day have behind them the reason why we do them; even the reason why we clean the house may not serve us. We can change the reason why we clean the home from 'because it is messy' to 'because of the freedom that a clean house gives'. This changes the reason behind the action from negative to positive, changes the energy that is generated and will in time change our attitude to doing it.

The Habit – The Magnet

Our habit gives us our expectations and conditions on how things should be.

The trouble with too much habit is that it makes us closed, unwilling to face the sense of vulnerability we feel when we open to the moment of the now. So we put our conditions and expectations on all that we see and do, thus maintaining the illusion that we know it all.

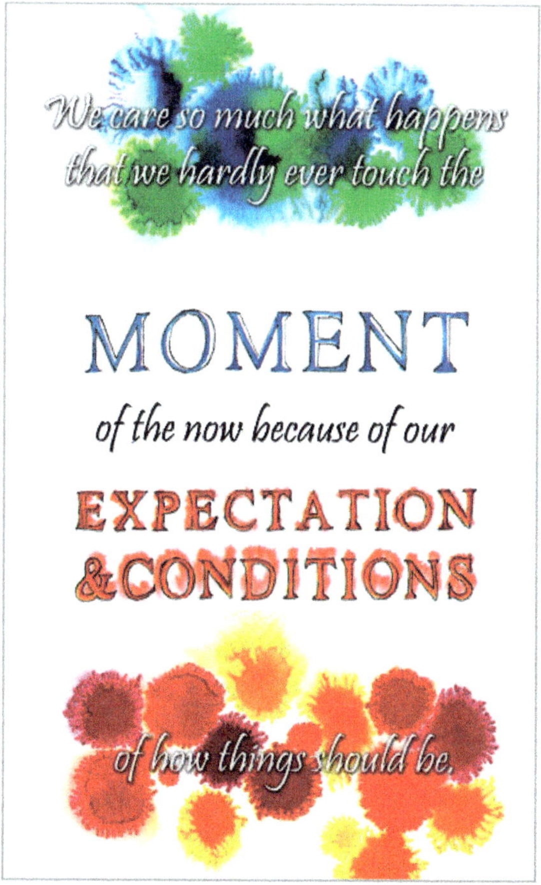

Being Open

To create and grow are fundamental parts of the meaning of life. It is what we are made to do and it is what the planet does so well.

The Habit – The Magnet

Finding ways to lift us above the expected

When the loves we feel about life cause us to step outside our habitual life and we create and grow in celebration of what we hold dear, we release an energy into ourselves that lifts us out of the expected into the realms of the unknown, and we become open again to the promise of life.

Habit	**The Magnet**
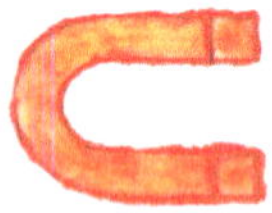	*Habit is the semi-conscious automated reaction to life according to personal history. It looks to ensure that our todays conform to our expectations and our prejudices of our yesterdays.*
Hero	*Glorious engine that will run without thought anything we repeatedly do.*
Villain	*When our habits propel us into our tomorrows with yesterday's meaning.*
Learning	*Just repeatedly do what you want to become.*

THE MIND

THE CRUCIBLE

The mind is a crucible of semi-conscious energies produced from our thinking, why we do what we do and what we feel about it.

Hero **Is capable of holding the enormity of the now.**

Oh, what a magnificent crucible of power the mind is, there is no truth it cannot hold, no precious moment that it cannot divine; it is the doorway to the universe and all that I can imagine!

Villain **When our mind is made up of things we don't value.**

Oh, what petty, trivial meaningless garbage my mind gives me to think about, an endless stream of divisive, critical and judgmental crap seems to pour from my mind about me and all that I see. And worst of all, it makes it sound like it's the truth!!!

Learning **The mind is loaded and directed by 'why we do what we do'.**

What is on my mind is there because of what I have asked it to hold for me. It's as simple as that!

Our thinking loads the mind with what things mean for us, the reasons why something is important.

Our mind is filled with the meanings we have given to our experience. These meanings tell the mind what is important to us and what is not; what it should be mindful about and what it should not. Why it is important depends on the reasons we have given it.

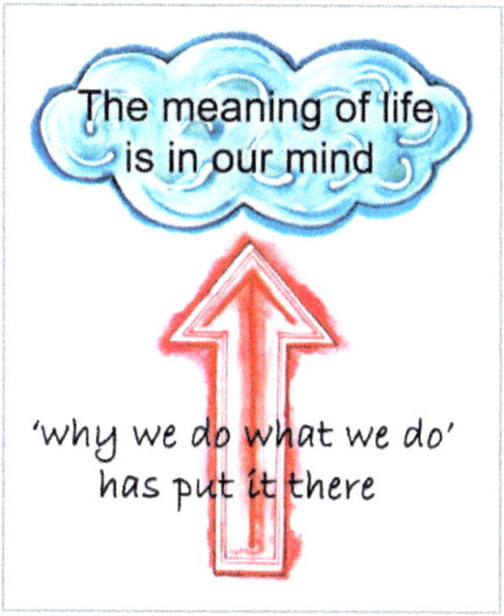

Behind the 60,000 thoughts we have every day are the reasons why we are thinking them. It's the reasons why we are thinking about the boss, money, dieting or going shopping that tells the mind what is important.

If we are thinking about money, our bank account, the bills we have to pay, the income from our job, and the overall meaning for us is 'not enough money,' then 'not enough money' is what the mind becomes loaded with –it's what is 'on our mind'.

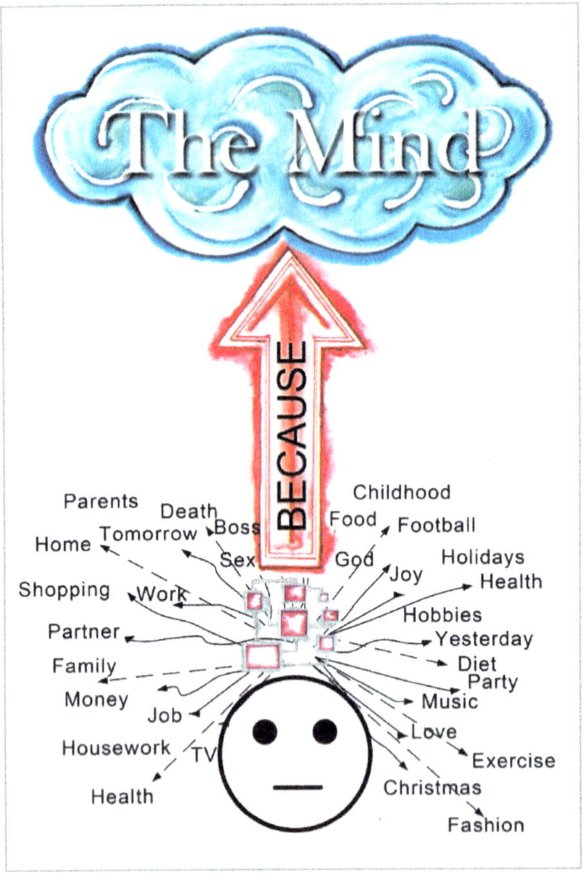

The Mind – The Crucible

The mind is filled with the cause of our thinking, the 'why' we are thinking it.

The mind does not listen to what we are thinking

listens to why we are thinking it.

The mind will then do its job and influence our thinking and awareness to more things that can be associated with the cause of our thinking, whether it be 'not enough money', insecurity, or gratitude.

The meanings we have about what we do are made important to the mind according to the amount of emotion, good or bad, we have about them. The stronger the emotion, the greater presence they have in the mind.

We have hundreds of things that have been made important in our mind, each one waving to get our attention, telling our mind where to go and what attitude it should take along with it.

These signposts we have filled our mind with are fine if they are harmonious and directing us on the road of our purpose, but if our deeper purpose in life is not present they can make our thinking chaotic with little rhyme or reason for who we love to be.

The meanings we give to our experiences over time become our beliefs.

The mind has a huge reservoir of 'what things mean for me' that has been created from our history. From childhood through to adulthood, we have had experiences that have formed the meanings and feelings we have about life.

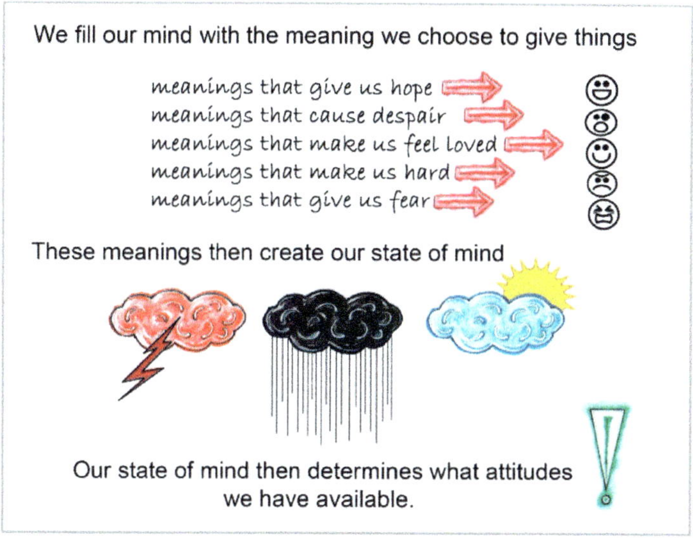

These meanings have, over time, formed our beliefs. Beliefs that we can, or can't, sing, draw, dance. That we are good or bad with money, the opposite sex, giving love. That we are a victim, God's gift to creation, a nobody. That there is not enough time, money or love to be who we wish to be.

The Mind – The Crucible

The mind creates our attitudes and prejudices according to meanings we have given to our experiences.

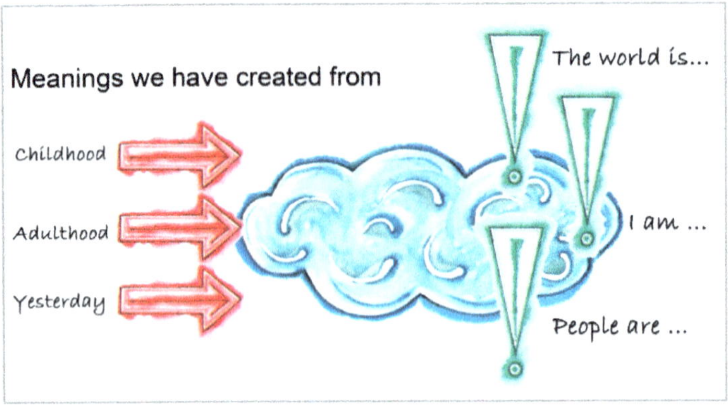

These beliefs, created in our yesterdays, have a profound influence on the attitudes we have available in our todays. The beliefs may or may not be useful, they may or may not even be true, but we have them and draw our sense of self from their presence.

What Makes Up Your Mind

Whether it's making up our mind to get out of bed in the morning or making a life-changing decision, it is the 'why' that makes up our mind.

Our state of mind is formed by what we have told it is important.

Our mind is heavily made up of the education of our teachers: the media, the commercial and business world, and the world of social conformity have all had their input, from looking cool to being rich, they have told us what is important and what is not.

This can leave our mind preoccupied with trying to not miss out and get more of what our teachers have said is important, what they continue to say we need to be happy. So the mind will dutifully produce the attitudes needed to 'win' in the battle to get the unimportant things that the world has made important.

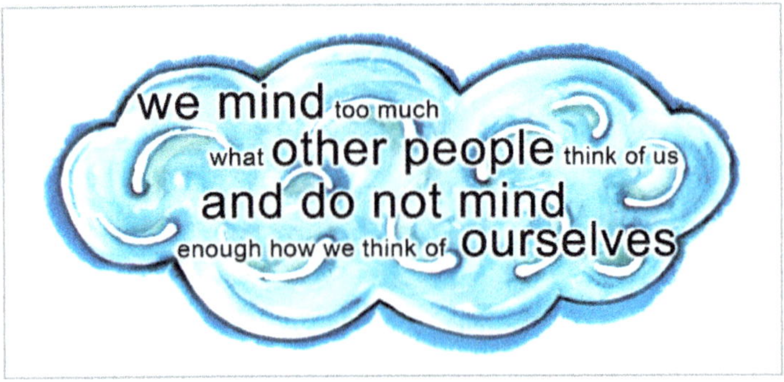

Integrity of the Mind

We draw our sense of self from our mind and become lost to ourselves if our reasons for doing things are not true to ourselves.

We will always struggle to feel our own authenticity if we make up our mind because of what is on the outside of ourselves, in pursuit of acceptance by others and the acquisition of things.

Although we can easily feel that our mind is at the beck and call of other people and the demands of the world within which we live, we are the author of our life and would, in truth, wish it to be no other way. Our authority is made manifest in the reasons why we do what we do.

The Mind – The Crucible

We can't be true to ourselves unless we care who we are being, who we are in relation to our deeper feelings about life.

Presence of Mind

Our real presence of mind comes from our authenticity, when we are being true to ourselves.

Although the mind has the capacity of living within the enormity of the now, we rarely give it the chance to do so. Our busy and crowded lives drive our mind to distraction with all the things we have and haven't done, all the things we should or should not do.

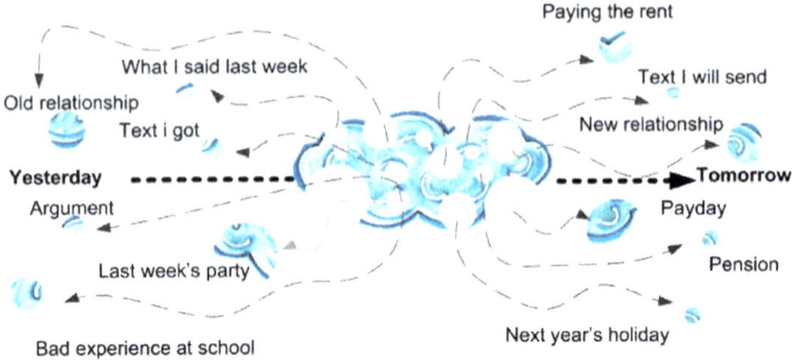

It is not often present. Instead, it is off chasing the things in our yesterdays and tomorrows that we have told it are important, frequently leaving us mindless in the now, just living off automated habitual responses to life.

We draw ourselves back to the now when we are at peace with ourselves, and the mind becomes unfettered from the threads from our yesterdays and tomorrows, allowing us to recreate our sense of self from the deeper meanings we have in life.

Keeping an Open Mind

Who we think we are is stored in the mind, made up from all the reasons why we do what we do.

We are very guarded in our self-view and become hostile if anyone challenges who we think we are. Yet most epiphanies, or life-changing perceptions, happen when a person has been forced, for whatever reason, to abandon their self-view; this may be from desperation, reaching rock bottom or from the shock of life-changing events. When this happens, when the mind can no longer rely on what it thought was true; it has to drop its expectations and conditions of how things should be and become open to what it does not yet know. In this open state we can create any picture we choose.

The Mind	**The Crucible**
	*The mind is a crucible of semi-conscious energies produced from our thinking, why we do what we do and what we feel about it*
Hero	*The mind is capable of holding the enormity of the now.*
Villain	*When our mind is made up by things we don't value.*
Learning	*The mind is loaded and directed by 'why we do what we do'.*

AWARENESS

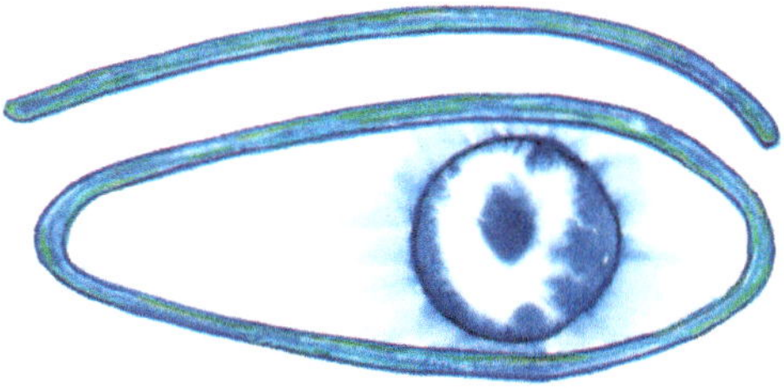

THE MIRROR

Our awareness is a mirror to our state of mind, a reflection of how we are feeling in ourselves. It is the mind's eye and sees things according to the energies, attitudes and purposes we are into at the time.

Hero **We can focus on peace in a world of chaos.**

Oh, I love my glorious awareness, how it shows me things that make me smile in the depth of me and fill my heart with hope! It can travel to the stars and the depths of the human soul; there is nowhere it cannot go.

Villain **When our awareness is fixed on what we no longer wish to see.**

It's like everything I see reminds me of it, like some bloody radar finding things that confirm my absence from the heart of me, confirming the ugly outside that I feel inside of me.

Learning **It shows us what we are connecting to, what we are feeding off and, because of that, where we are going.**

I have learnt, as much as I can, to be aware of my awareness, because it is telling me who I am being and because I do care who I am, I am able to read the signs my awareness is telling me.

Our awareness is an unbiased faculty of perception that is made biased by our conditions and expectations of how things should be.

The meaning we draw from what we see is a mirror to who we are being.

Things Go with Things

A dress designer is aware of the dresses, a plumber is aware of the plumbing. If we are feeling sorry for ourselves our awareness of the world seems to confirm why we should feel sorry for ourselves.

Our awareness picks up anything that is on the same frequency we happen to be on that hour, day, year, life. If we have anger, our awareness will pick up on more things to be angry about. Hope finds hopeful things.

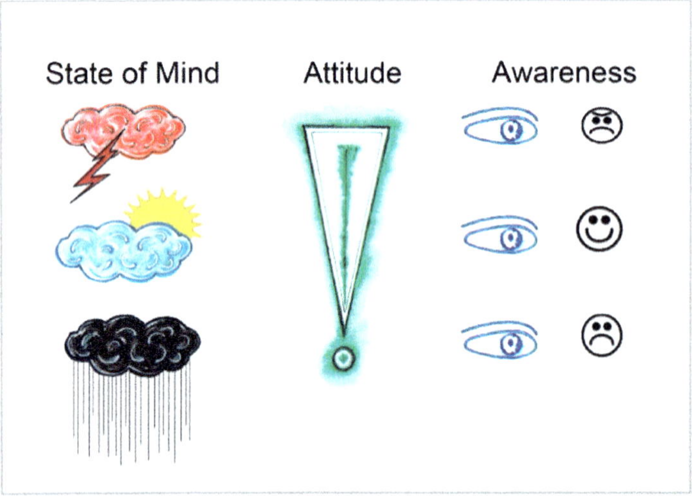

We can't see things that don't go with the energy we are running on: we can't see hope in despair, we can't find love in fear, we can't know peace when we are wanting more!

It's what's important and why it's important that drives our awareness.

Where our awareness goes and what it sees is determined by our attitude, our attitude is caused by our current state of mind, our state of mind is created by what we have deemed important and the reasons why we think it.

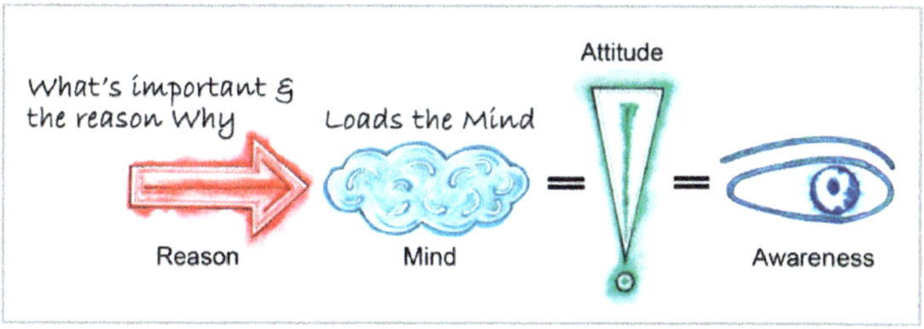

Our awareness mostly runs at a semi-conscious level. Driven by habit, it rushes around like a pin ball, bouncing from one thing to another according to the likes and dislikes we have created about life. We hardly ever see anything for its own sake, we only see what it means according to the prejudices we put upon it.

The Gentle Habit of Self-awareness

Learning to become aware of our awareness is a great skill; it allows us to know who we are being and because of that where that being is taking us.

Self-awareness allows us to know ourselves, it gives us wisdom in our attempt to look after our well-being – but self-awareness is tricky. We think we are our awareness and so become personally involved in all that we see. We have hosts of things we like and dislike, created from our history, that are ready to jump upon what we see, eager to name and shame everything as right or wrong, good or bad, better or worse.

The more we can develop a gentle self-awareness, the more we create the ability to change our relationship to our awareness, from being the punter at the front row of the cinema of our awareness to being the film director, directing our awareness from our conscious purpose of who we wish to be.

Levels of Awareness

Our awareness is such a dynamic faculty; it is useful to have a simple self-awareness location tool to help understand where our awareness is at and how our awareness changes according to where we are in ourselves.

	Awareness	Emotion	Thinking
	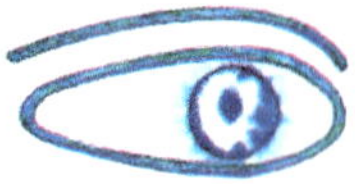		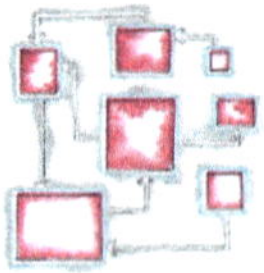
	Aware of	Feelings of	Thoughts that
Essence	The union of things	Gratitude	Allow
Values	The Meaning of things	Appreciation	Assess
Things	The Separation of things	Personal likes and dislikes	Judge

Our awareness changes according to whatever energy/reasons are driving us at the time.

There are different levels of awareness: awareness of things, awareness of the meaning behind the things and awareness of the essence of things.

Level of Things

At the level of things, our awareness is mostly driven by our habits; it just runs along in the background directed by our habitual responses to life. So we see the same things in the same way. We hardly ever stray off the well-worn paths of our comfort zone. It is to do with things for things' sake, a confirmation of the commercial world and our habitual response to the needs of earning a living and all their ramifications. We are aware of the noise of life with little reference to its deeper meaning other than how it relates to getting by. There is no pause for self-reflection and little sense of appreciation except for our own gratification.

At this level, our awareness only confirms the separation between things. We don't connect to what we are seeing, we impose preconceived views and interpretations upon our awareness according to how we think things should be. We may see a tree and say, "A tree, an oak tree" – we do not feel it, do not connect to it. We may see another person and name them as short, tall, fat, pretty, well dressed or badly dressed, but we do not feel the life of that person. We become like a pinball that rushes around the table just bouncing off one thing after another.

Level of Values and Learning

At this level of awareness we move away from the unimportant noise of life. We become more aware of the rhyme and reason of things, the cause and effect of what is going on, the energy behind the action, the person behind the face, the atmosphere or aura of a place or thing.

We connect with what we come across, drawing meaning and learning according to the deeper values we have about life.

What we see at this level inspires creativity, allowing us to contribute to the meaning of life.

When we are at this level of awareness we can feel our heart's presence and can tap into its blessing.

Our self-awareness at this level allows us to know ourselves, and we become more aware of the causes of our attitudes and actions, not what person or thing caused them but what it is in us that gave them permission to happen. Forgiveness and gratitude are easy to bring into being at this level because our well-being becomes paramount.

'Is'ness – Connecting to the Essence of Things

This state of awareness sees and allows the flow of life and acknowledges that 'what is, is'. It is non-judgmental and has no wish to label things as good or bad, better or worse. It has a compassion that comes from knowing that all things are connected and all are sister or brother. It allows us to feel the essence of things, the core qualities of a person, place or ourselves.

It brings a settlement because we become aware that we need nothing more than to be who we are.

While I stood there I saw more than I can tell and I understood more than I saw for I was seeing in a sacred manner the shape of all things in the spirit and the shape of all shapes as they must live together like one being. – *Black Elk*

Awareness	**The Mirror**
	*Our awareness is the mirror to our state of mind. It is the mind's eye and sees things according to the energies, attitudes and purposes we are into at the time.*
Hero	*It shows us what we are connecting to, what we are feeding off and because of that where we are going.*
Villain	*When our awareness is fixed on what we don't want to see.*
Learning	*We can focus on peace in a world of chaos.*

REASON

THE DIRECTOR

Reason is the 'why we do what we do'. It is the motivation for our thoughts and actions. It gives direction to our lives.

Hero **We draw our nourishment and create the meaning of life from the reason why we do what we do.**

I feel the meaning in all that I do. The rhyme and reason makes sense to what I love, I am a giant! I feel invincible with a power that can move mountains and a vision that can touch the furthest horizon.

Villain **When the reasons we do things no longer fill our heart.**

I feel bereft of power, nothing gives nourishment and nothing stops the erosion of my will. I wonder why I even bother to get up in the morning, there is no point, there is no real meaning other than to 'get by', to get through the day again!

Learning **We can choose any reason for anything we do.**

When I am feeling lost I use the reason why I do what I do to reconnect me to a source of meaning that makes sense to who I love to be, that allows me to remember what is really important.

I want ... Because ...

We carry many 'wants' in our life, both short term and long term. We may want to go shopping, go on holiday, make love, more money, peace and quiet, or a partner. Behind the 'wants' we feel in life exist the reasons why we want them. These reasons are the power that drive us and give direction to our lives; they are the purposes we have that hour, day, year, life.

The reasons may be conscious or habitual; they may be because of vengeance, gratitude, guilt or care. Because of fear of tomorrow or the love of the moment. The list is endless, but whatever the reasons we have for what we do, somehow, somewhere we have decided upon it, given it permission to be the director of our lives at the time.

We live in a busy world that gives us many different reasons for 'why we do what we do'. This, coupled with our ever changing self-view according to whether we feel we are winning or losing in life, can cause the purpose behind our reasons to be at best inconsistent and at worst chaotic and confusing.

The noise from all our different reasons often makes for a discordant sound, with little rhyme or reason for our deeper purpose in life.

If there was some great god capable of granting our wishes, they would have great difficulty in knowing what it was that we really wanted. They would not know if we really meant what we said because we say we want so many different things and what we say we want changes so often.

This is not true for those that have a passion in life. It permeates all that they do. They have constancy about 'why they do what they do' and the great god (who is them!) understands the meaning and grants the vision, wisdom and will to achieve their love.

The purpose of life is in our heart and we have known it all along.

We carry in our heart a singular reason for living, to express the loves we feel about life and to release peace and happiness because of it. It's not that we don't know this, it's just that the way of the world makes it so easy to forget, it makes it so easy for the unimportant to become important.

We can create reminders about the deeper meanings we have about life. We can change the direction the signposts are pointing so at least we end up in the vicinity of our deeper values of life.

Types of Reason

The power behind the reason determines the choices we make.

There are different types of reason why we do what we do. We can work out what we should do and the logical reason why we should do it, but still not be bothered to do it. We can be enthused about what to do and the reason seems clear, but the following day or week it no longer moves us – and yet sometimes we just know we will do it.

The heartfelt choice is true integrity; the others only recreate the illusion of choice.

Lots of thinking, little feeling – I should!

These reasons are dry, intellectual and have little feeling. They may have clever thinking but no heart. They are often brittle and inflexible.

Little thinking, lots of emotion – I must!

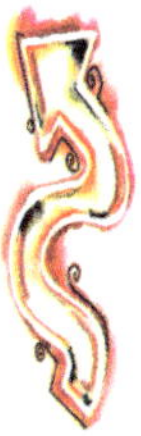

These reasons move us on a Tuesday, but may not be there on a Friday. They are built on shallow emotion or other people's emotion and because of that, they have weak vision and comprehension about the purpose at hand.

Heartfelt understanding – knowing – I will!

Experiencing these reasons causes a presence of mind about what we are doing. They are felt in the depth of ourselves and come with an intuition and a vision that inspires and encourages us.

We can't lie to ourselves. Something inside of us knows when we mean what we say, all the rest is just 'perhaps', 'should', 'ought', 'maybe' or 'seems like a good idea'.

We Get What Our Reason Is Asking For

Why we do what we do is the causal essence of our actions; it is the frequency of the signal we are sending to ourselves and the world about who we are and the world cannot but respond accordingly.

Reason - why we do what we do

is our call to the law of attraction

We attract to ourselves whatever goes with the 'meaning we have in the feelings' about what we do.

We Cannot Attract What We Don't Have

You can't win the lottery without buying a ticket.
You can't sing a song without knowing the tune.
You can't feel compassion in arrogance.
You can't feel hope in despair.
You can't give care with impatience.
You can't have fear in love.
You can't learn without being open.
You can't laugh in depression.
You can't be at peace wanting more.
You can't grow in yourself without gratitude.
You can't live in the now with regret.
You can't be happy without being at peace with yourself.

The Feeling from the Meaning

We live with the meanings we have given to our past experiences and the feelings that those meanings evoke. From childhood to our current age we have had hurts and loves that have created the meanings we have given to life.

These over time have become our beliefs about what is and what is not important in life. They have become part of the driving force of who we are today. They are the stories we tell ourselves about the world and who we think we are.

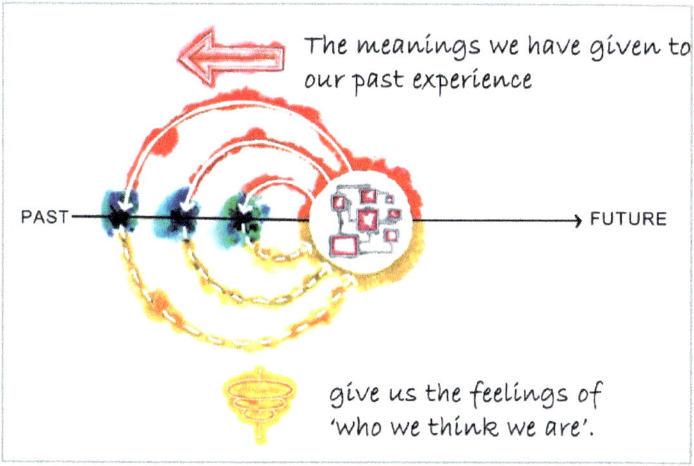

The feelings we get from our experience are because of the meaning we gave it at the time. They were reasonable given what we knew and felt at the time, but may not be true given what we now know; they may not be useful or reasonable according to what is important now in our lives.

If we change the meaning,
we change the feeling.

The meanings we have from our past are not fixed; they change according to how we think about them.

We can, if we choose, give our past experiences any meaning we want, and in so doing we change the feeling we get from it.

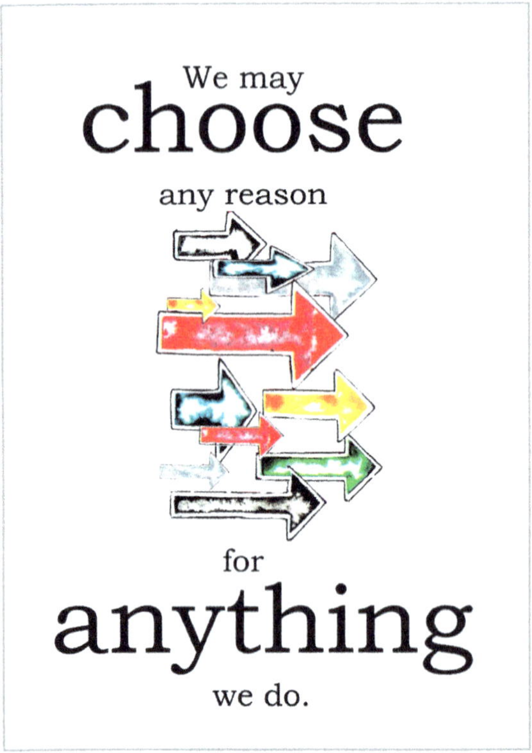

Whose Reason Is It Anyway?

When we are sharing the loves we feel about life, it brings us back to the deeper reasons we have for living. We become settled with ourselves, all is forgiven and we are at peace and happy because of it. But we can lose trust in ourselves and turn to the world outside for a motive for our actions. When we do this we abandon our authenticity for the thousand and one reasons for doing things that the world has given us that have little to do with the heart of ourselves.

Our authenticity is within the reason why we do what we do.

We are the authority for our life. We choose who we will be, what we will do and the reason why we will do it. We live a self-choosing, self-creating life and would wish it to be no other way.

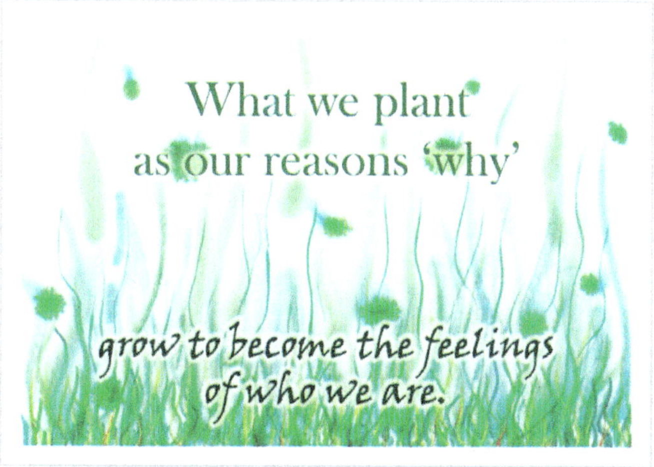

Our sense of self, 'who we think we are', has been created from the thousands of 'why we do what we do.' These are the messages we have told ourselves about who we wish to be.

Reason – The Director

Of all the powers we have been given, our ability to choose why we do what we do is the most profound; it is the light and the beacon that guides our destiny.

Reason is great for getting there; it is no good for being there.

Although reason is a great tool for creating our future and provides us with the security of knowing why we do what we do, living a life of pure reason leaves no room for the unknown, and there is more in life and within ourselves that is outside our current reasoned perception. Reason and thinking rarely go with intuition, gut feelings or great creativity.

Sometimes 'no reason' is a good reason for doing something.

To be able to act outside of our box of reason is a powerful ability. It requires courage to step away from the security that our reasoned thinking gives us. It also requires trust that we can cope with the unknown. But it is always within the space of the 'unknown' that great lives are made.

Reason	**The Director**
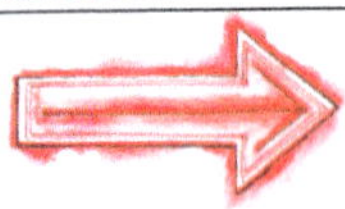	*Reason is 'why we do what we do'. It is the motivation for our thoughts and actions; it gives direction to our lives.*
Hero	*We draw our nourishment and create the meaning of our life from the reasons why we do what we do.*
Villain	*When the reasons we do things no longer fill our heart.*
Learning	*We can choose any reason for anything we do.*

ATTITUDE

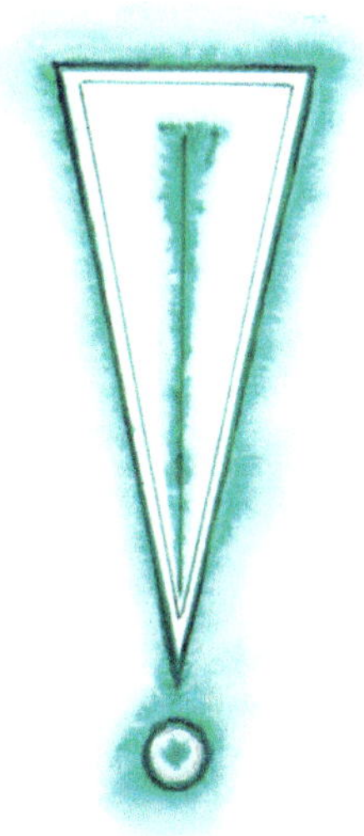

THE CONDUCTOR

Our attitude is the expression of our state of mind. It sets the tone of our engagements with life. It conducts the many parts of ourselves according to who we see ourselves to be.

Hero **There is no attitude we cannot assume if we so choose.**

When my attitude is beholden to no-one but my own heart, there is no-one I cannot be, no door that cannot be opened. I am as I was made to be: free.

Villain **When our attitudes belong to everyone but our own heart.**

I am lost from myself, no longer true to what I love, alone and adrift in a sea of other people's expectations and the endless demands of the world; I thrash about trying to grab something, anything that will stop me sinking deeper into the petty attitudes that the world seems to think are so important.

Learning **Our attitude is the gatekeeper that manages the doors of what we believe can and can't be done.**

I have learned that my attitude is everything, that if I want an attitude that nourishes my life I need to cherish myself because if I can't love myself I can never really love another or life itself!

Our attitude can raise us up to the level of the gods and can dash us upon the rocks of despair. It can climb mountains, heal our body, create a masterpiece or bury us in self-doubt. It commands our willingness and our ability to learn. It can make an easy job hard or a hard job easy. It is born from how we see ourselves and it conducts our awareness of the world.

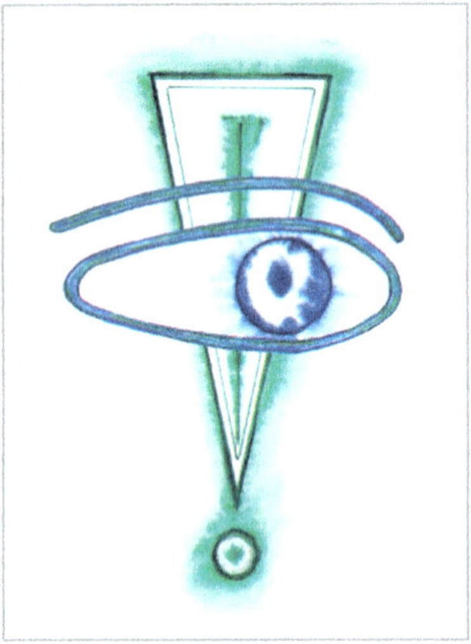

Our attitudes determine what paths we take and what paths we avoid. They have been built from the aggregated meanings we have given ourselves about all aspects of life, from the face in the mirror, to Mondays, to sex, to our job – even to the washing up!!

Our attitudes are the gatekeepers managing the doors of what we believe can and can't be done.

We have created hundreds of attitudes about all aspects of our life. To things like spiders, sport, fashion, food and money. To people and groups like rich people, poor people, fat people, disabled people and ethnic groups. To the world in general: "It is a hard place", "It's out to get me", "It's an opportunity". And attitudes about ourselves: "I am bad at ...", "I always ...", "I am ...", "I can never ...".

Our attitudes are a reflection of our state of mind.

They are born in us because of what things 'mean' for us. The greater the meaning something has for us, the stronger the attitudes we have about it. If we don't mind it doesn't matter! But if we do mind, then it does matter and our attitude and actions condense around what we have deemed important.

Whose Attitude Is It Anyway?

It is accepted social behaviour to blame other people and things for how we are feeling in ourselves. This creates the belief that our attitudes are caused by other people and the things that are going on in our lives. So we blame society, our parents, the government, religion, the next-door neighbour, even the cat for the attitudes we have. But the point of our attitude is that it is 'our' attitude, no one else's. We have given it permission, for whatever reason, to appear in our life. We may justify it by blaming other people but this only gives other people authority over who we are. This is neither wise nor true and more importantly, it isn't useful.

If your attitude is not happy, it doesn't mean that if you take responsibility for it, you become happy, it just means you know where you can go to change things –you!

Our attitude is born from the choices we have made, for whatever reason, about what things mean for us.

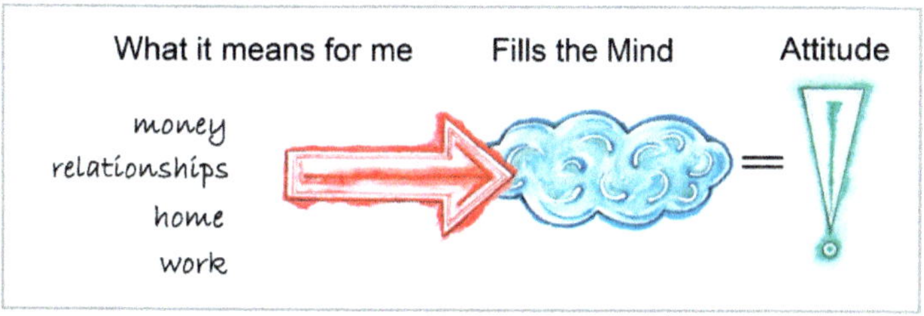

The meanings we carry around in our mind about life define who we think we are.

Who we think we are determines the attitudes we have available to deal with the world and ourselves.

We have created our attitudes because of the meanings we have given to our past experience. These attitudes, over time, become etched into the face and may show caution, willingness, anger, sadness, suspicion or fear. So the world is approached with this attitude, and our awareness ensures that we get back from the world whatever our attitude is attracting. Anger will find anger, fear will find things to be fearful of and an optimistic attitude will allow us to see things to be optimistic about.

Reasons

Our mind is loaded with the meanings
we have given to our experience.

The Mind

Our state of mind gives us our
attitudes about what we are facing in life.

Attitude

Awareness

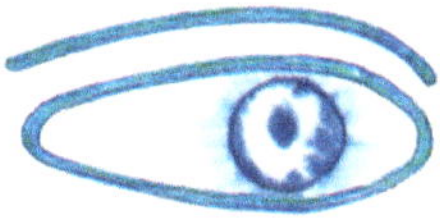

Our attitude then conditions
our awareness to what we see and do not see.

Creating an Attitude

Our attitude is an end result, a reflection of our state of mind.

To change your attitude, change your mind.

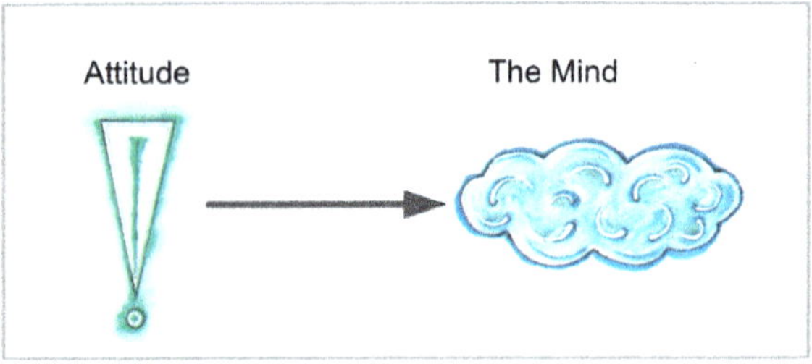

If we want to change our attitude about a person, ourselves or the world, we need to change our mind about it. We need to make up our mind differently about what it was that allowed the attitude to form in the first place.

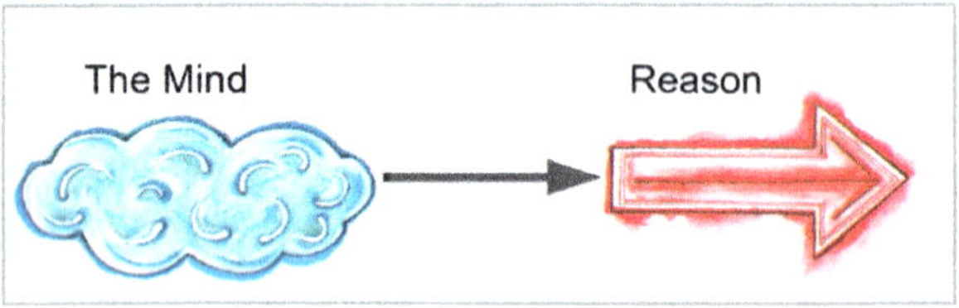

To change your mind, change your reason why.

We have made up our minds from the meanings we have given to our experience, the reason why something is important to us and the reason why we do what we do.

If we change the reason, we change our mind. Our reasons were, after all, just a conclusion we came to with the reasoning we had available at the time.

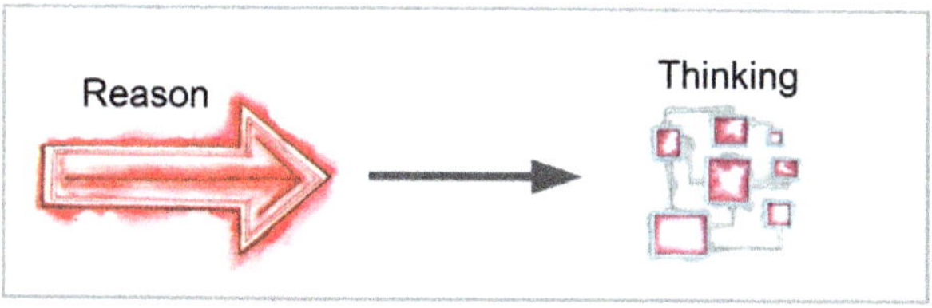

To change your reason, change your thinking.

To be able to change the reason why we do what we do, we have to change how we think about it, bring different associations of 'what goes with what', to cause different things to come to mind when we think about ourselves, another person or the world.

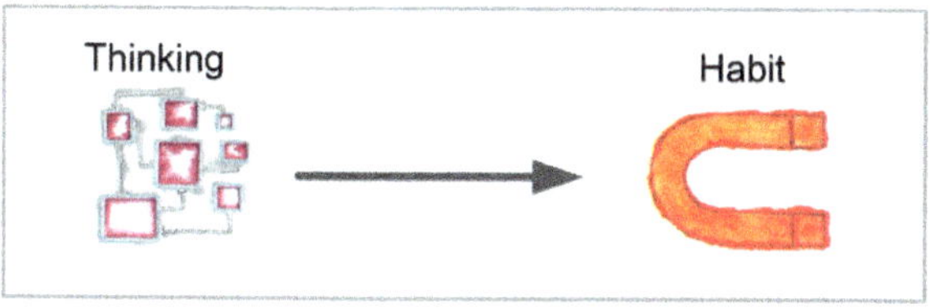

To change your thinking, change your habits.

To be able to change our thinking, we have to change our associations of what goes with what. We have to come from a fresh place in ourselves, a place that is not dominated by the comfort zone of yesterday's habitual thinking.

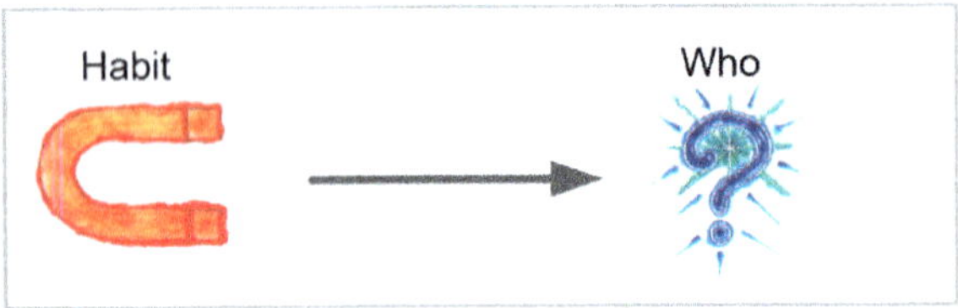

To change your thinking habits, you have to change who you think you are.

To change the habitual view of ourselves, we have to go to a place in our self that has the freedom, power and flexibility to do so: the place that holds the deeper values and loves we feel about life, whatever they may be.

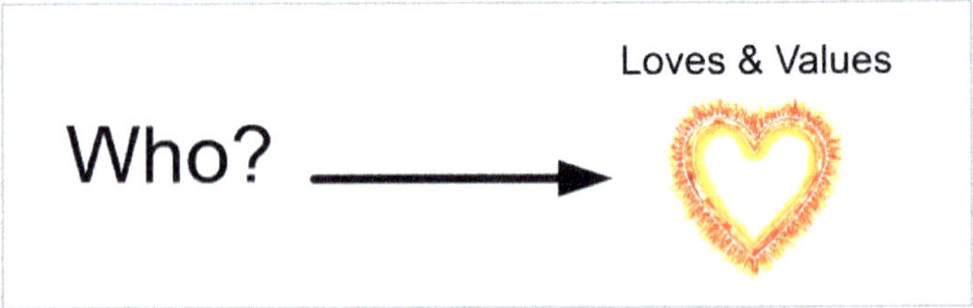

To change who we think we are, we have to go back to the very heart of ourselves, to the core of what is truly important to us. This has the power to bring us back into the truth of who we are and give us the unrestricted vision of what is possible.

We can never have a truly sustainable positive attitude if our attitudes are at the beck and call of other people and the ever-changing weather of our circumstances. If the reference for who we are is in what other people think of us or whether we are winning or losing in our conformity to the accepted norm, we will always be willing to abandon the truth of ourselves. The only place we can go in ourselves to find a truly sustainable attitude is the heart of ourselves.

Attitude	**The Conductor**
	*Our attitude sets the tone of our engagements with life. It conducts the many parts of ourselves according to who we consider ourselves to be. It is the expression of our state of mind.*
Hero	*There is no attitude we cannot assume if we so choose.*
Villain	*When our attitudes belong to everyone but our own heart.*

INTUITION

THE MESSENGER

Our intuition is the net of semi-conscious enquiry that we are constantly sending out into the world.

Hero **The door to more than we can imagine.**

My intuition gives me a thousand threads to worlds beyond my education, from the life of a tree to the feelings from the stars. There is nowhere it cannot travel, no picture it cannot show me.

Villain **When our intuition is driven by selfish gain and the fear of losing out.**

When I am lost and struggling to keep my sense of 'I' of who I think I am, my ego will usurp my instinct making me see where and how I can win in the ludicrous game of power struggle with others.

Learning ***Our curiosity, wonder and awe make us open to its guidance.***

I have learnt that the intuition is a real faculty of understanding. So I find ways to abandon my preconceived views on what I see, to listen to its guidance and have the courage to step into the unknown.

Intuition The Messenger

Our intuition gives us tuition about life without prior knowledge, or discernible reason. It is a knowing that has not been tamed by our thinking and reason.

We struggle for clarity in our lives, to understand what is happening, why it's happening and what tomorrow may bring. So we turn to the 'gods' of thinking and reason to understand the world within which we live, and they provide us with 60,000 thoughts every day in our attempt to live and plan our lives. As impressive as they are in coping with the everyday demands of the world, we have another faculty of understanding available to us that can, in a fraction of a second, bring us a huge amount of information from the look of another person, a view of the stars or a feeling about a future or a past event.

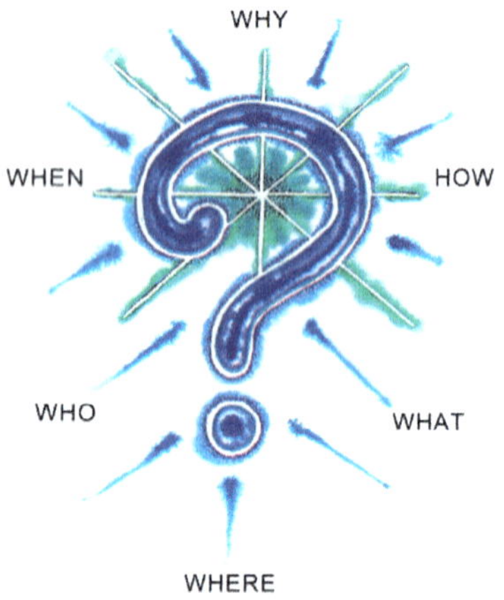

Our thinking and reason are great tools for helping us make sense of the world but they are slow and clumsy in comparison to the intuition.

Our intuition is much maligned by the world because of its intangible nature and is sidelined by the dominance of our thinking. Yet it is what we turn to when our thinking and reasoning has used up all its options and is the guiding light for all creative people.

Intuition defies logic and reason. There is no logic in the gut-feeling we sometimes use for our decisions. There is no known reason why we should get a feeling about a person we have only just met, or knowledge we may have about a future event.

Our intuition, that at one level can be seen as a faculty of the instinct, is constantly 'out there' checking out what is going on and giving us back semi-conscious knowledge about a person, place or thing.

is a knowing
untamed by our thinking and reason.

*Knowing the majesty
of nature in a sunset.*

*Knowing a life story
in a look.*

Knowing love in a caress.

*Knowing the purpose we
hold in our heart.*

Our intuition is in the feeling or knowledge we get about a person, place or thing or what direction to take when we are lost.

We use our intuition when we take a 'wild guess' or follow a gut feeling. We use it whether we are asking ourselves about the meaning of a beautiful sunset or when the next bus is coming.

Our intuition does this reading of people and places all the time. If we get something back from it, we look to clothe it with reason. We look to the physical world for confirmation of our intuition. So we read the person's posture and face, or we look to understand the architecture of a building or room. This clothing of our intuition is useful but we did 'get' something before the reason and thinking took over.

Our Web of Intuition

Our intuition flows strongly through our threads of empathic connections.

Our intuition is not limited by time and space. It can give us knowledge about a person we care for who is hundreds of miles away and give us feelings about how tomorrow will be.

Our homes are full of things that hold meaning for us, connections to memories, to the values and hopes that we have in life. There may be pictures of loved ones, memorabilia from foreign travel, books that hold stories that move us, objects of sentimental value, pictures that represent hopes and aspirations. We have threads to all these, consciously or unconsciously.

Things can pull on our threads and names, places and experiences from our history can pop into our minds for no apparent reason. For instance: an urge to visit a place or to contact a friend. So we pick up the phone and call the friend who keeps popping up in our mind, they are most glad we rang because they are going through a tough time. We visit the place we felt drawn to and benefit from the experience.

Levels of Intuition

The range that our intuition works on is massive, and because it is such an ethereal subject it is useful to separate out different aspects of our intuition.

The Messenger

We get thousands of intuitional messages everyday giving us tuition about what is going on behind the physical appearance of things.

The messenger is the intuition we send outward to a person, place or thing, either by our unconscious instinct or by our conscious curiosity. It then gives us tuition back that is beyond our physical perception.

When we meet someone for the first time or enter a building or room, our instinct sends our intuition to check it out, to get information about the person or place. This may give us a feeling about a person or about the atmosphere of a place or building.

What we get back from our intuition is a knowledge that may make us feel comfortable or uncomfortable with the person. We may feel dragged down or lifted up by the atmosphere of the place.

Knowing the messenger puts us in touch with the unseen worlds, the cause of the physical appearance of things. The more we become aware of this intuition, the more our focus changes from the end results to the cause of what is going on, the energy behind the action.

The Oracle

This level of intuition allows us to know what will be because of what was; it gives us an awareness of the rhythm,
flow and pattern of things.

The oracle of intuition gives accuracy in our anticipations of what will be, like knowing something is going to happen when we feel the energy before a storm.

It knows the picture of what will be because it is in touch with the pattern of what was. Like a musician who is feels the rhythm and flow of an essence and describes it in music, the painter who feels the power of nature and describes it with colour, texture and pattern.

When this intuition is turned inward to ourselves, we become aware of the energy we are processing, the rhythm and reason of who we are and because of that, we see what we are attracting to ourselves, what can and cannot happen because of the song we are singing.

The Guide

The Guide of intuition connects us to the actuality of the moment, the power of now and the deeper truth of what is going on.

This is an inward tuition that helps us listen to the song of our heart, our heartfelt feelings about life. It is like a guide dog that can take us safely on our journey in life when we can't see the way. It has our best interests at heart, helps us avoid dangers and gets us to places in the world and in ourselves that can allow our loves of life to be expressed.

The intuition is a gentle voice that can't be heard over the noise of our stress and anxiety.

The more we build a true compassion for ourselves, the more we learn to trust the Guide of intuition.

Being Open

Intuition is what we use to connect to the moment of life, the power of the now, where the thinking and reason can't go.

When we can quiet our own chattering story of what we think should or should not be, our intuition can direct our awareness to see things in a light other than that of our own prejudices.

We are in truth, with all things, and the flow of knowing never ceases. We just can't hear the stories that are being told to us because of our obsession with our own story.

Our intuition is activated whenever we have curiosity, wonder or awe, whenever we make ourselves open. Gratitude is a powerful way to re-create our natural openness to life, and love is the ultimate essence that allows us to see and feel the deeper meanings of life.

Intuition	**The Messenger**
	*Our intuition is the net of semi-conscious enquiry that our instincts and mind are sending out into the world.*
Hero	*The door to more than we can imagine.*
Villain	*When our intuition is driven by selfish gain and fear of losing out.*
Learning	*Our curiosity, wonder and awe make us open to its guidance.*

Hero & Villains Summary

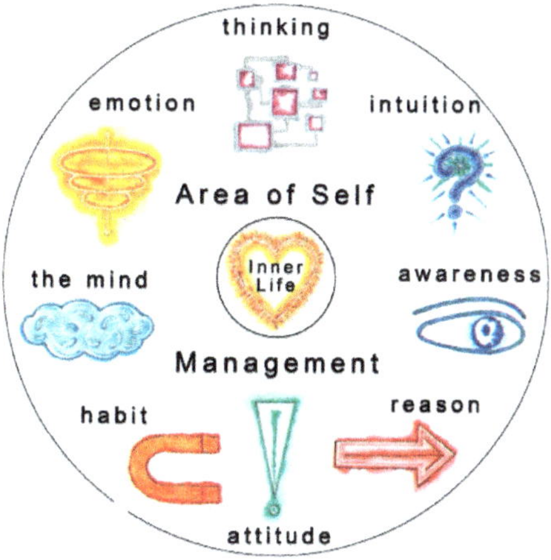

These are the players within our area of self-management; they create our world, bring harmony or discord to our lives. They are the resources we have to determine our future and give our life meaning. They are servants to the heart of us, to the deeper purposes we feel about life but can only serve us according to how we have educated them.

Much of this education has been created by the demands of the world upon us and has produced a life of habitual living with little time or inclination to release our own unique path of creativity and healing. It's too easy to just follow others and do what has been done before.

How do we break the cycle of habitual behaviour and bring light to the heavy parts of us, create enough strength in us that it is easy to touch again our love of life?

There are two journeys that will do this. The first is created in the outer life of us, in the actions and attitudes we use to create our world; the second is within our journey to the inner life of ourselves, in the building of our relationship to ourselves. Although the inner journey to self-love will bring everything, it is assisted and made pleasant by the actions we do in the outer life, in building the bridge that allows us to move from a life of general habitual living (the grumpy and boring), to the inspired life of ourselves.

The bridge

There is a bridge that we can create between our maintenance life and our inspired life, a bridge that allows us to remember who we love to be. It allows us to forget the things we don't want to remember and remember the things we don't want to forget. It is built from the attitudes and actions that cause our heart to soften and our mind to open.

When I am in the mundanity of life, I can't see or feel the wonders that I have when I am inspired; it seems a universe away, a lost dream, and no amount of huffing and puffing or whinging seems to bring it closer.

When I am in my inspired life, I cannot understand why I don't go there more often. It's obviously the best place to be and getting there seems so simple!

I have learnt that there is a bridge that gives access to the inspired life, a bridge that is not difficult to create. It may require a little effort and a little courage, but it never fails because it is built with things that allow a smile to appear in myself again.

Our life can appear very unstable at times; our ability to hold our heartfelt values of life and the picture of who we wish to be weakens and strengthens with every shiny or dull thing that catches our attention.

We can be in our inspired life one day, feeling the glory of the moment and the vision of our beloved future. The next day we can become reduced to the mundane. The maintenance life and the general habitual living we have to do to survive in the world, the job, the housework, the bills and all the other things we need to do in order to get by in life. This can cause the love we felt when we were in our inspired life to appear like an illusion, a forgotten dream.

The three lives

Although we can get overwhelmed by the never-ending 'to do' list of the maintenance life, its purpose is to create the space and opportunity to get at the creative, caring and sharing life of ourselves (the building life) and so ignite our inspired life.

The maintenance life

The maintenance life is to do with everything we have to do to maintain our life, to keep it in good working order so that we can get at and release our heartfelt purpose in life. Its range is vast and includes looking after our body, paying the bills and sorting our head out to get on with the day.

We have a hundred and one things that we need to do to just get by in life, and a hundred and one things that the commercial and business world demands that we chase in order to fulfil their requirements of us. There is so much to do to it is easy to be drawn into the illusion that this is all there is, that moments of creativity, peace and happiness are the whim of the gods or are to be obtained from the standard drugs of the 21st century: the TV, the internet, alcohol, shopping etc.

The absence of the healing qualities of the inspired life or the building of self-worth that happens in our building of life, makes it easy for unimportant things in life to become important and important things to become unimportant. So we end up thinking that what other people think of us is more important than what we think of ourselves, that the things we have are more important than the feelings we have and that what is happening on the outside of ourselves is more important than what is happening on the inside of us.

Although most of the energy that is produced in this life is dominated by our habits and reasons that do not belong with our heart, we can we can use these same powers to create habits and reasons that allow us to remember what we don't want to forget.

The building life

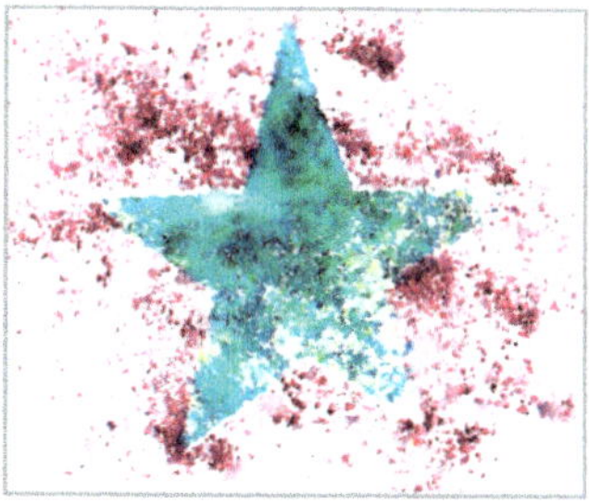

The building life generates the attitude, energy and opportunities to escape the mundane and feel again the possibility of our inspired life. It is our life of exploration, creativity, learning, caring and sharing. Things we do in this life allow us to heal our past, build the future and open the door to our inspired life. When we do things in this life it makes us feel whole and allows us to smile again at our heart's purpose.

There are thousands of things we can do in the building life: we may clutter-clear the house, do gardening, go skating, sing, dance, meditate, go for walks in the country, whatever allows us to again feel gratitude about life. Whatever the building block you choose, remember why you are doing them and do them long enough so they become a habit.

The building life is divined by asking yourself what you do or can do that causes your heart to soften and frees your mind. Whatever it is, it will make you smile at yourself, feel loved and allow you to remember who you love to be.

This is one of the greatest wisdoms a person can ever find for themselves because the answers are the building blocks of the bridge to an inspired life and the sign posts to your soul journey on the planet.

Inspired life

When truly we love who we are, we feel the humanity in all that we do, and we become our part again in the moment of life.

This is the life where we let go of who we think we are and join in the moment of life. We become graced by the power to create our life anew. We connect to our heartfelt values in life and feel the deeper meanings of all that we see and do.

When I manage to let go of the unimportant things that my mind seems to be preoccupied with, and I escape the oppression that my expectations and conditions give me about how things should be, I have the chance to touch the moment of the now, to slip into a world where there is no distraction from my vision of what is possible. I feel my heart rejoice and I feel my soul breath deeply in the light that this freedom gives.

When we are in this life we fill up our well of well-being and nourish the parts of us that have been starved by the dominance of the maintenance life.

There is a natural wish to share the healing that is created in this life.

The perceptions we see in this life allow us to see what is truly important and what is not; it gives us inspiration about our building life, the things we can do and create that give opportunities to return again to our inspired life.

The inner world – learning to love yourself

Our ability to release the heroes and heal the villains of ourselves resides in our self-love, in our ability to connect to the heart of ourselves, wherein lies the greatest source of happiness and healing.

Self-development without self-love creates a tyrant to ourselves and to others. It has no real compassion and no ability to see the true meanings of life. Without self-love we live in the shallows of life and do not see the causal essence of things – this insight is reserved for those that are in touch with their own causal essences, their hearts.

Our relationship to ourselves is the most important relationship we will ever create; the absence of a healthy relationship brings a mountain of stress, anxiety and pain. It makes our response to what happens in us and around us something we orchestrate by fear rather than compassion or love. But the upside of loving ourselves is enormous; it brings happiness, compassion, well-being and above all a wish to be true to our heart's purpose and our soul calling. Because as we learn to love ourselves, we pave a way to the heart of ourselves, unlocking a powerhouse of creativity and well-being.

Self-love can be tough because we have to be soft to the parts of us that make us hard.

We are so many people, the grumpy me, the child me, the dumb me, the angry me, the quiet me, the lost me, the found me, the laughing me and the crying me.
So, so many people.
The me that does not give a shit, the me that cares too much, the me that sings with the stars and the me that grovels in the mud. Oh what a family I am, such a gathering of people. And somewhere within it all are the thousand chinks of light and the hundred distant lanterns that light our way.

It's easy to love ourselves when we are feeling good, but it's tricky when we are feeling bad, and it can seem impossible when we are feeling ugly.

We do not love the grumpy of us, the sad part of us, the hostile part of us, the parts of us that act as if we do not care. We name them as 'not us' and so drive a sword into ourselves, separating ourselves into the good and the bad, the worthy and the unworthy of ourselves. We declare this part of ourselves as a 'disturber of the peace', a foe to our purpose, an antagonist to our harmony, and so we become the intolerant parent to the hurting child within us, the part in us that is in distress, in need of understanding, in need of love.

We are, after all, the whole of ourselves. We can't abandon who we are nor can we drag a part of us kicking and screaming into our future; it will only be a troubled journey with little peace.

Learning self love is a journey to reunite the family of ourselves, to make us whole again. It gives us back the wisdom, power, and the creative vision that can only come from a unified self. It allows us to forgive ourselves for all the things we did or did not do and lift the weight of all the things that may or may not be. It will dissolve our fears and replace the illusion of our fragility with a beautiful sense of vulnerability that connects us to the deep of ourselves and all that we see.

Self-Love is the subject of my next book to be published in 2018

Our task in life is not to learn but to liberate what we love in life. (We may learn because of it but without our heart, self-learning is an illusion.)

Lightning Source UK Ltd.
Milton Keynes UK
UKOW06f0705280517
302091UK00014B/87/P

9 781909 465411